THE SUMMER BEFORE FIRST GRADE WORKBOOK

parragon.

Helping Your Child

- Remember that the activities in this book should be enjoyed by your child. Try to find a quiet place to work.

- Your child does not need to complete each page in one sitting. Always stop before your child grows tired and come back to the same page another time.

- It is important to work through the pages in the right order because the activities get progressively more difficult.

- The answers to the activities are on pages 124–128.

- Always give your child lots of encouragement and praise.

This edition published by Cottage Door Press, LLC, in 2020.
First published 2017 by Parragon Books, Ltd.

Copyright © 2020 Cottage Door Press, LLC
5005 Newport Drive, Rolling Meadows, Illinois 60008

Written by Nina Filipek, Anita Loughrey, and Catherine Casey
Cover art by Irina Avvakumova, used under license from Shutterstock.com
Illustrated by Simon Abbott and Adam Linley
Educational Consultant: Marla Conn, Read-Ability, Inc.

All rights reserved. No part of this publication may be reproduced, stored in a retrieval system, or transmitted, in any form or by any means, electronic, mechanical, photocopying, recording, or otherwise, without the prior permission of the copyright holder.

ISBN: 978-1-68052-994-4

Printed in China

Gold Stars™ is an imprint of Cottage Door Press, LLC.
Parragon Books is an imprint of Cottage Door Press, LLC.
Parragon® and the Parragon® logo are registered trademarks of Cottage Door Press, LLC.

Contents

Phonics and Spelling	4
Reading and Language Arts	36
Math	66
Space, Measurement, and Time	96
Answers	124

Phonics and Spelling

Helping Your Child

- The activities in this section will help your child to learn about phonics and spelling. Pictures provide hints and clues to support their understanding.
- Your child will gain the confidence to sound out letters and begin to decode words.
- Your child will learn about consonant sounds, beginning and ending sounds of words, long and short vowels, letter combinations, and word families.
- Set aside time to do the activities together. Do a little at a time so that your child enjoys learning.
- Give lots of encouragement and praise.
- The answers are on page 124.

Contents

Word Endings	6
Vowel Sounds	7
More Vowel Sounds	8
Making New Words	10
Describing	11
Last Sounds in Words	12
Word Pairs	13
Adding the Letter e	14
Groups of Words	15
ch, sh, and th	16
ch and sh Sounds	17
Say the Sounds: ch, sh, th	18
Trace the Letters	19
Rhyming Words	20
Match the Rhyming Words	21
Letter Blends – Beginnings	22
Letter Blends – Endings	23
Vowels and Consonants	24
Say the Sounds: wh, ph	25
Say the Sounds: ai, a–e	26
Sounds the Same	27
Say the Sound: ea (short sound)	28
Say the Sound: i-e	29
Say the Sounds: ee, ea	30
Magic e	31
Say the Sounds: ow, oa	32
Say the Sounds: oo, ou, u	33
Say the Sounds: ar, or	34
Find the Rhyme	35

Word Endings

Draw lines to connect the words that have the same endings.

ball

balloon

bee

nail

carrot

tree

snail

wall

moon

parrot

Vowel Sounds

Draw a circle around the correct middle sounds.

a / o 	i / u 	o / a 
i / e 	i / e 	a / u 
u / a 	o / a 	i / a 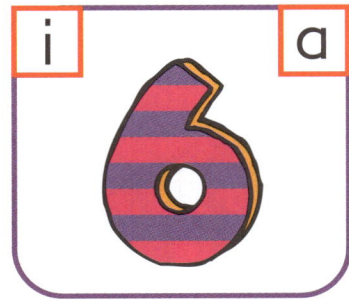

Note for parent: Ask your child to name each picture to help them with this activity, listening to the letter sounds as they say each word.

More Vowel Sounds

Use the vowels **a, e, i, o,** or **u** to complete the words below.

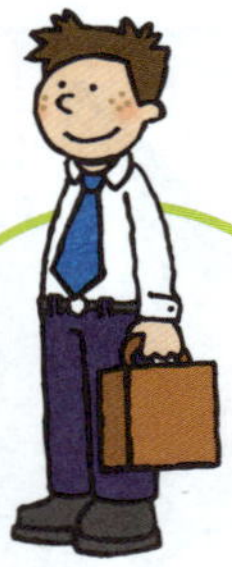

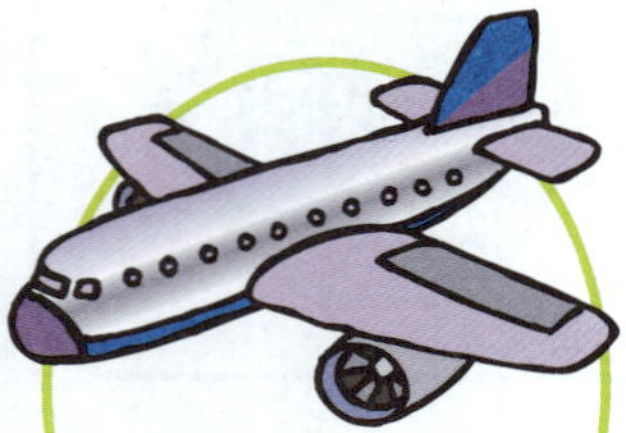

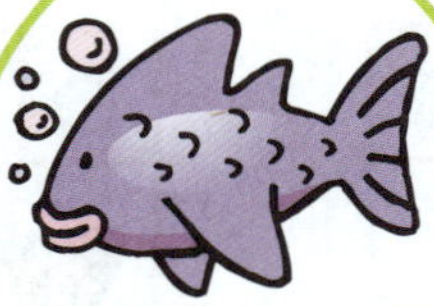

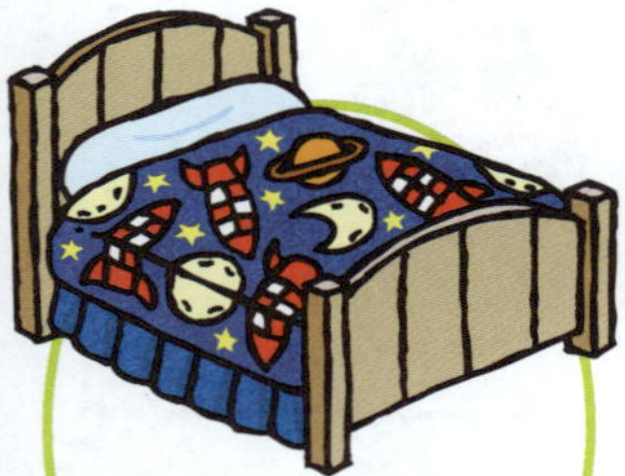

- m_n
- r_d 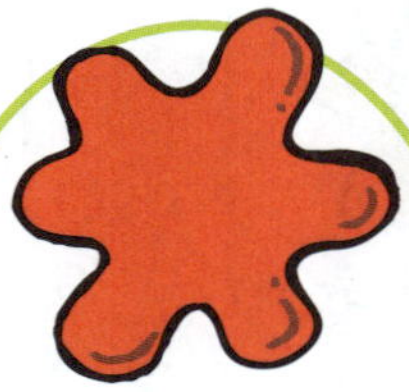
- p_g 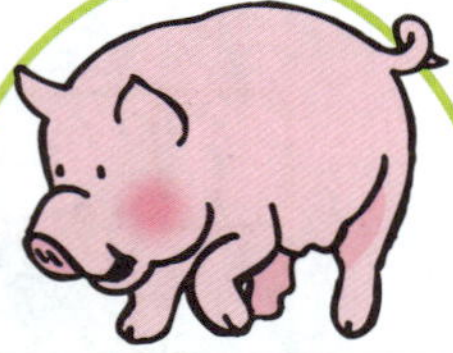
- s_ck 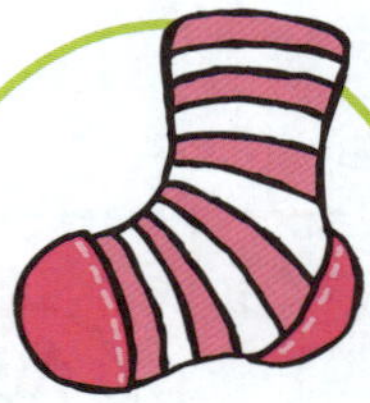
- j_t
- d_ck 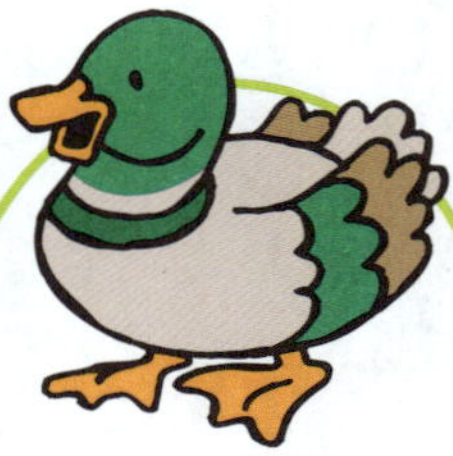 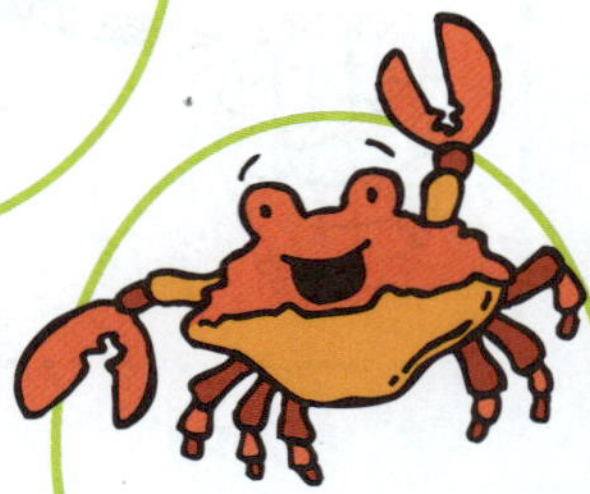
- b_s
- cr_b
- b_d
- l_g 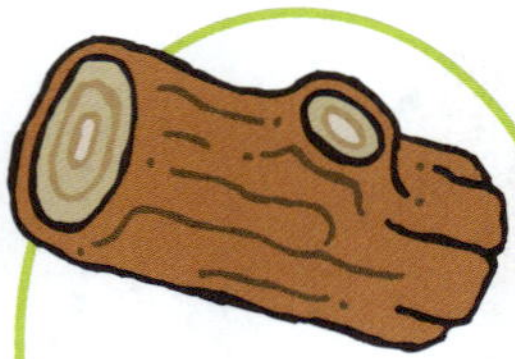 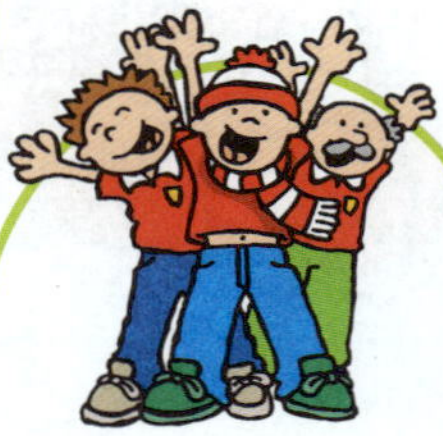
- f_sh
- m_n

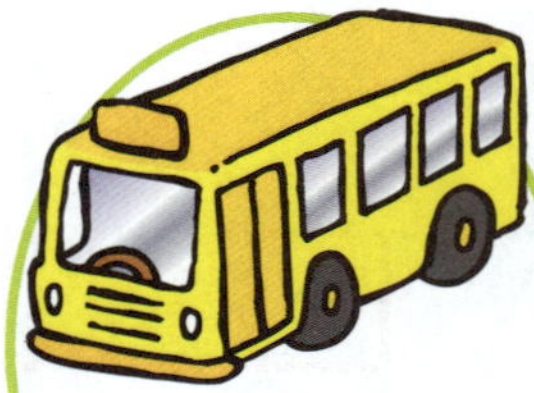

Write the middle letter next to the picture, then connect the pictures that have the same middle sounds.

Making New Words

Write the new words you make.

Change the b in bat  to make c _ _

Change the f in fox  to make b _ _

Change the j in jar  to make c _ _

Change the d in dog to make l _ _

Now draw a picture of each new word and write them in the boxes below.

_ _ _

_ _ _

_ _ _

_ _ _

Describing

What are these sentences describing?

Choose a word to write at the end of each one.

> shorts   sheep   shark   shoes   ship   shell

1. This sails across the sea. _ _ _ _

2. You find this on a farm. _ _ _ _ _

3. You wear these on your feet. _ _ _ _ _

4. This fish has very sharp teeth. _ _ _ _ _

5. You find this on the beach. _ _ _ _ _

6. You wear these in the summer. _ _ _ _ _ _

Note for parent: This activity helps with understanding and spelling.

Last Sounds in Words

Say the name of each picture. Write the last letter sound at the end of each word.

 bu _

 do _

 ba _

 dru _

 cra _

 for _

 cu _

 te _

Note for parent: Children need to listen carefully to identify last letters.

Word Pairs

Write the last sound in each word. Choose from this list. Draw a line to connect the words that have the same ending.

ck sh ch ar

s o _ _

f i _ _

b r u _ _

w i t _ _

c _ _

d u _ _

s w i t _ _

s t _ _

Note for parent: This activity helps your child to learn about the word endings ck, sh, ch, and ar.

Adding the Letter e

Add the letter **e** to the end of each word to make a new word. Write the new word and draw a picture of it.

cub

_ _ _ _

pip

_ _ _ _

fir

_ _ _ _

cap

_ _ _ _

Note for parent: This activity helps your child understand what happens to a vowel sound inside a word, when an e is added to the end.

Groups of Words

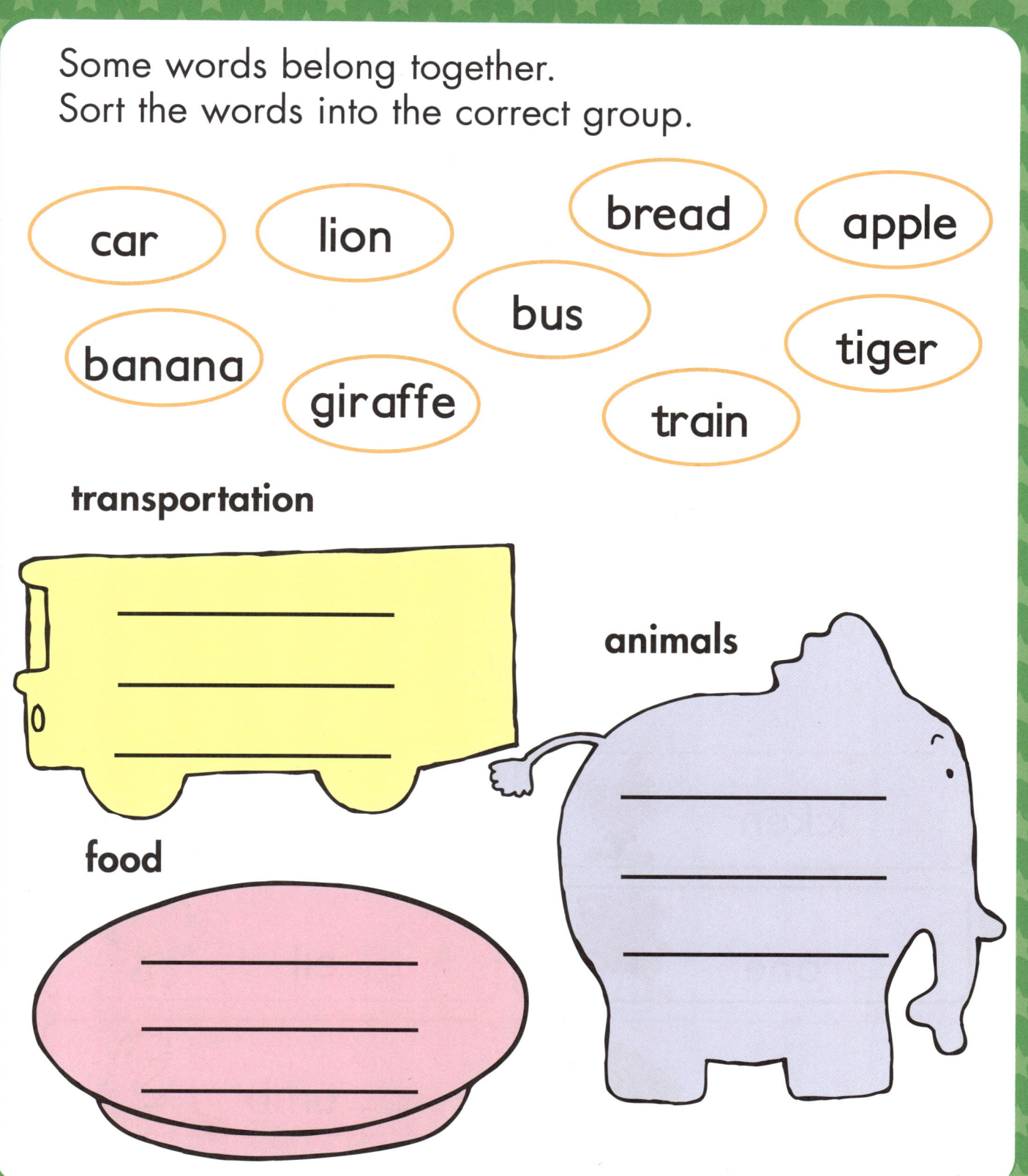

ch, sh, and th

Say:

Read the word endings below. Choose the correct letters to complete each word. Write the letters on the lines.

ch   sh   th

__ __ icken

__ __ ip

__ __ rone

__ __ ell

__ __ eese

__ __ umb

Note for parent: Help your child to read each of the word endings, then choose the correct starting sound. Help them write the letters in the spaces.

ch and sh Sounds

Say the word for each picture. Draw lines to connect each picture to the correct beginning sound.

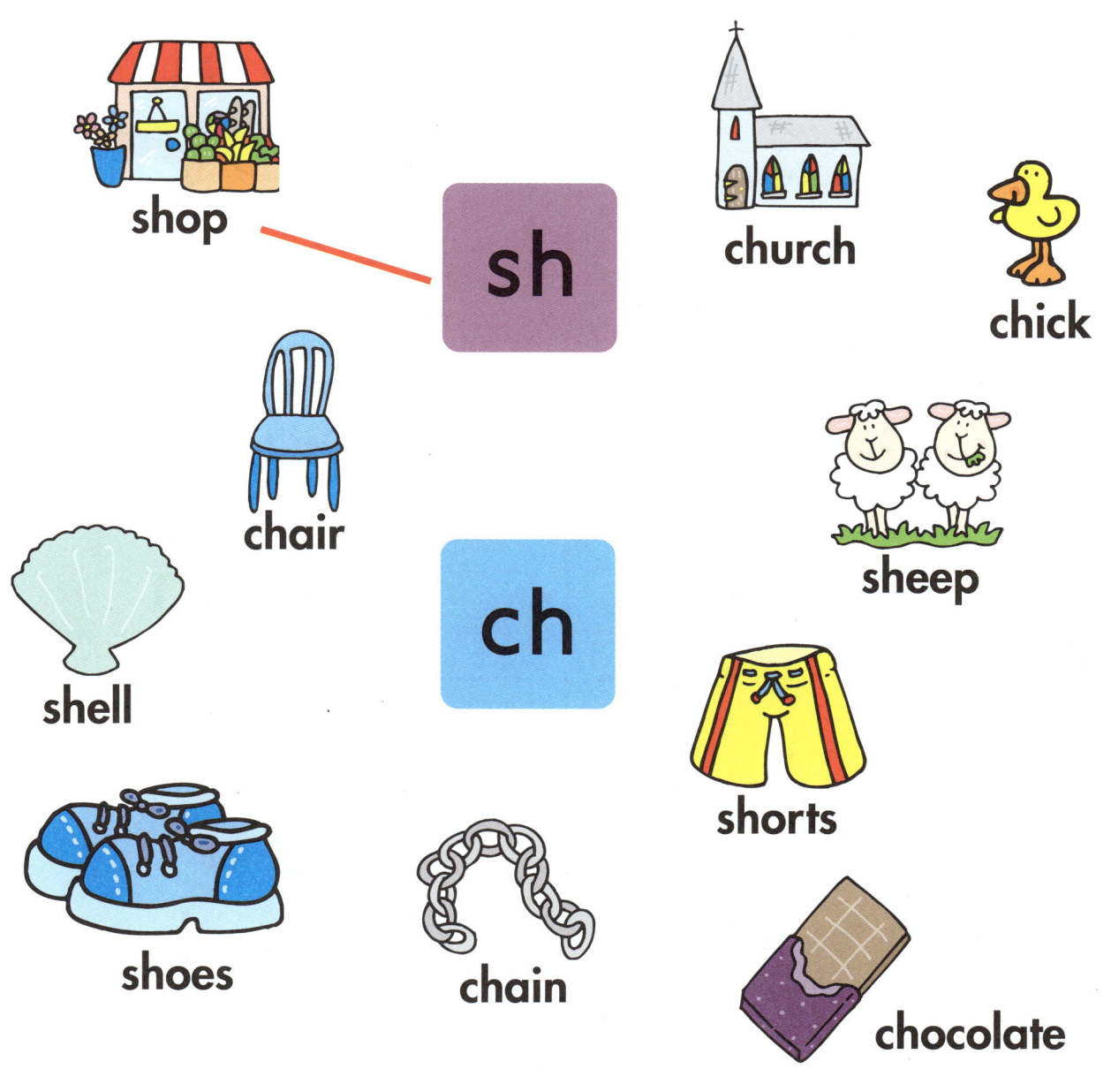

Note for parent: This activity helps your child to learn that two letters can make one sound. It gives them practice in distinguishing between ch and sh sounds.

Say the Sounds: ch, sh, th

Say the name of each picture. Circle the sound you can hear in each word.

ch or sh

ch or th

ch or sh

th or ch

th or sh

th or ch

Note for parent: This activity introduces common consonant digraphs. A digraph is two letters that together make one sound.

Trace the Letters

Trace over the letters.

ch　　sh　　th

Trace the letters to complete the words.
Read the words.

dish

think

thick

shop

chill

ship

chip

rush

thin

wish

chick

shed

Note for parent: These common digraphs can appear at the beginning or the end of words.

Rhyming Words

Read these words out loud. For each colored box, write more words that rhyme in the spaces.

| bug  |
| mug |
| |

| jar  |
| car |
| |

| hat  |
| bat |
| |

| ten  |
| hen |
| |

Match the Rhyming Words

Draw a line to connect each rhyming pair.

clock

phone

chick

lock

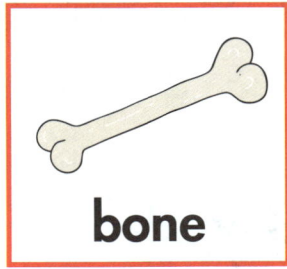
bone

light

night

stick

Note for parent: Challenge your child to think of more words that rhyme with each rhyming pair.

Letter Blends – Beginnings

Blend the sounds to read the words below. The first two letters make one sound.

For example: **fr-og**

Try these:

- cr-ab
- gr-it
- fr-et
- gl-um
- gr-ab
- sn-ub
- tr-oll
- sn-ug

Note for parent: The first two letters in these words are consonant digraphs. Together they make one sound.

Letter Blends – Endings

Blend the sounds to read the words below. The last two letters make one sound.

For example: **ju-mp**

Try these:

- la-mp
- ye-lp
- si-nk
- ca-rd
- di-sk
- bu-mp
- so-ft
- de-sk

Note for parent: The last two letters in these words are consonant digraphs. Together they make one sound.

Vowels and Consonants

The alphabet has 5 vowels. They are: a, e, i, o, u. Find the vowels and color them in red. The other letters are called consonants. Color these in a different color.

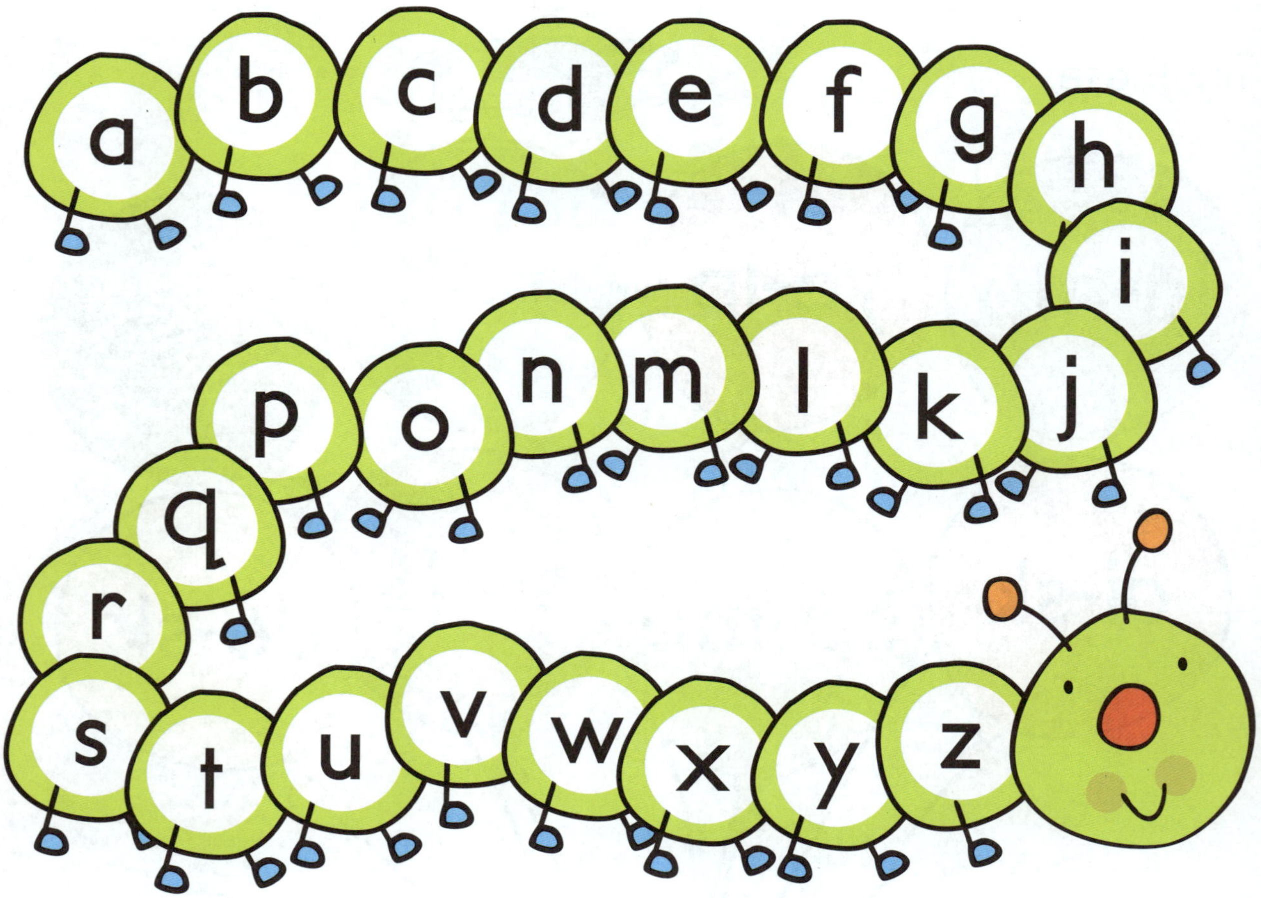

Write your name in the space below—with each letter in a circle. Color the vowels in your name in red and the consonants in another color.

Note for parent: Your child needs to know what the vowels and consonants are. Most words in the English language contain vowels and consonants.

Say the Sounds: wh, ph

Say the sounds of the letters. Trace over the letters.

wh for

ph for

photo

phone

whizz

when

whisk

wheel

graph

whip

whim

whale

white

phonics

The **wh** sound begins lots of question words: what, when, where, why?

Note for parent: Point out that the digraph ph sounds like f.

Say the Sounds: ai, a–e

Blend the letter sounds **a** and **i** to read these words.

r-ai-n

ch-ai-n

tr-ai-n

These words have the same long sound of **a** but are spelled differently.

m-ane

pl-ane

cr-ane

Draw lines to connect each picture to a word.

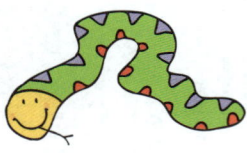   

snail   lake   gate   snake

Sounds the Same

Words can sound the same but have different meanings.

For example:

> A squirrel has a long (tail).
> This is a fairy (tale) book.

Circle the words that sound the same but have different meanings.

> Tim has a pain in his knee.
> This is a window pane.

> A town has a main street.
> A male lion has a mane.

Note for parent: Words that sound the same but are spelled differently and have different meanings are called homophones.

Say the Sound: ea (short sound)

Trace over the letters.

ea   ea   ea

Write the letters **ea** in the spaces to complete the words. Read the words.

sleepy h_ _d

brown br_ _d

light as a f_ _ther

blue thr_ _d

winter w_ _ther

green m_ _dow

Draw the missing pictures to match the words.

Say the Sound: i-e

The **e** at the end of these words changes **i** from a short sound into a long sound.

Say these words:

| pin – pine | pip – pipe |

Write **e** at the end of the words, then read them aloud.

strik_

slic_

ric_

mik_

lik_

ic_

bik_

hik_

nic_

trik_

Note for parent: Sometimes the e at the end of these words is called magic e because it changes the sound of the vowel that comes before it.

Say the Sounds: ee, ea

The letter-sounds **ee** and **ea** often sound the same. For example:

I can see a spider.

I can see the sea!

They sound the same but have different meanings.

Say this rhyme.

A sailor went to the sea sea sea,
To see what he could see see see,
But all that he could see see see,
Was the bottom of the
deep blue sea sea sea!

Note for parent: Follow the words with your finger. Point out that see and sea sound the same but are spelled differently.

Magic e

Write **e** at the end of these words to make new words.

plum_ spin_ ton_ rob_
can_ cap_ cut_ cub_
hug_ plan_ tap_
tub_

Note for parent: Here are more examples of magic e.

31

Say the Sounds: ow, oa

Trace over the letters to write the sounds in the words. Read the captions. Draw the missing pictures.

billy goat

long coat

warty toad

rowing boat

deep snow

dog show

bow and arrow

flower growing

Note for parent: Notice that flower is a different **ow** sound.

Say the Sounds: oo, ou, u

Trace over the letters to write the sounds in the words. Read the captions. Draw the missing pictures.

Good book

Take a look

I can cook

Big truck

Best of luck

Beans and jelly – yuck!

Trace over the letters to write the sounds in the words. Read what the children are saying.

I could.

He would.

You should!

Say the Sounds: ar, or

Read the words. Listen for the different sounds of **ar** and **or** in these words.

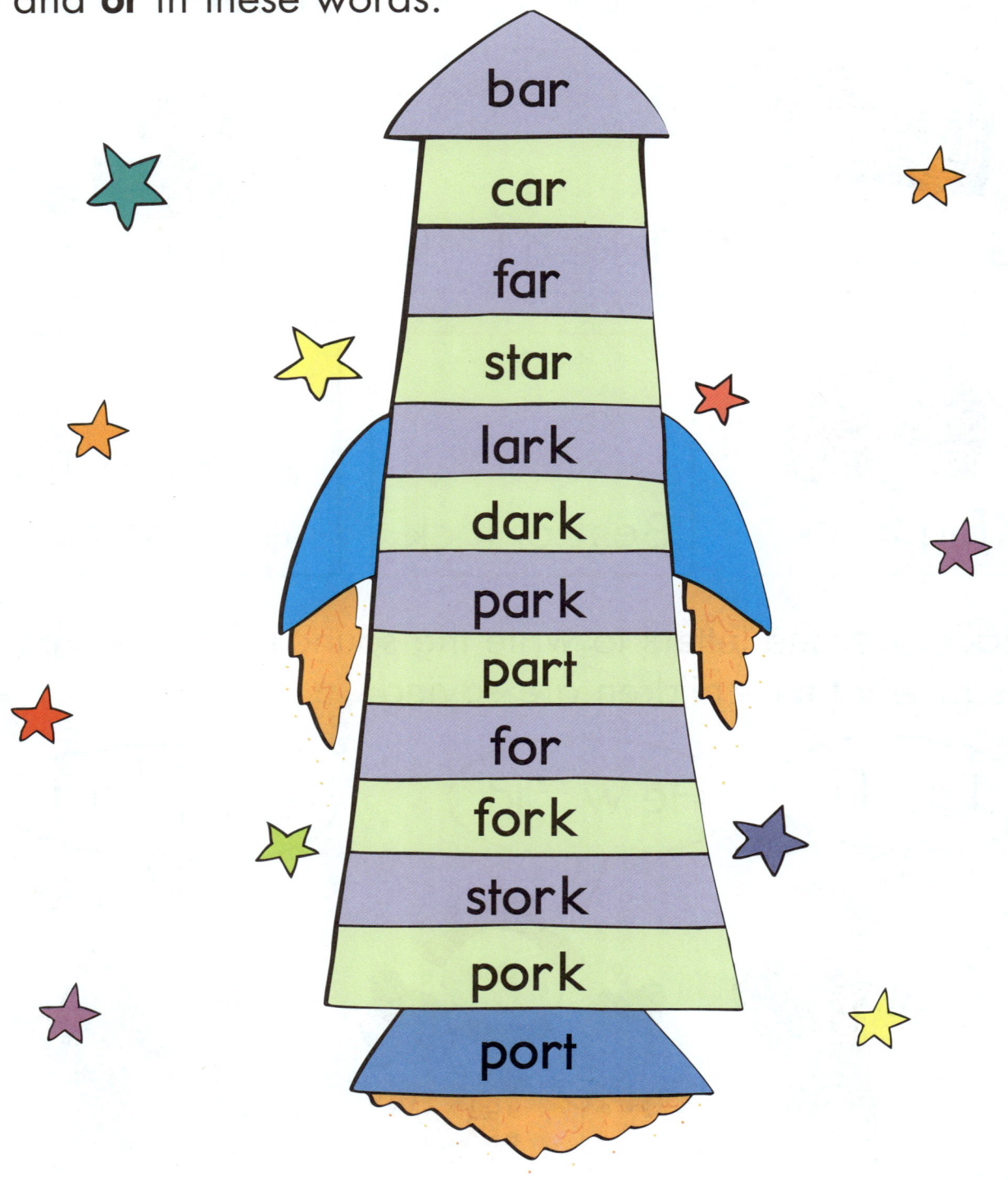

bar
car
far
star
lark
dark
park
part
for
fork
stork
pork
port

Note for parent: Help your child to read these words. Follow the words with your finger. Listen for the differences.

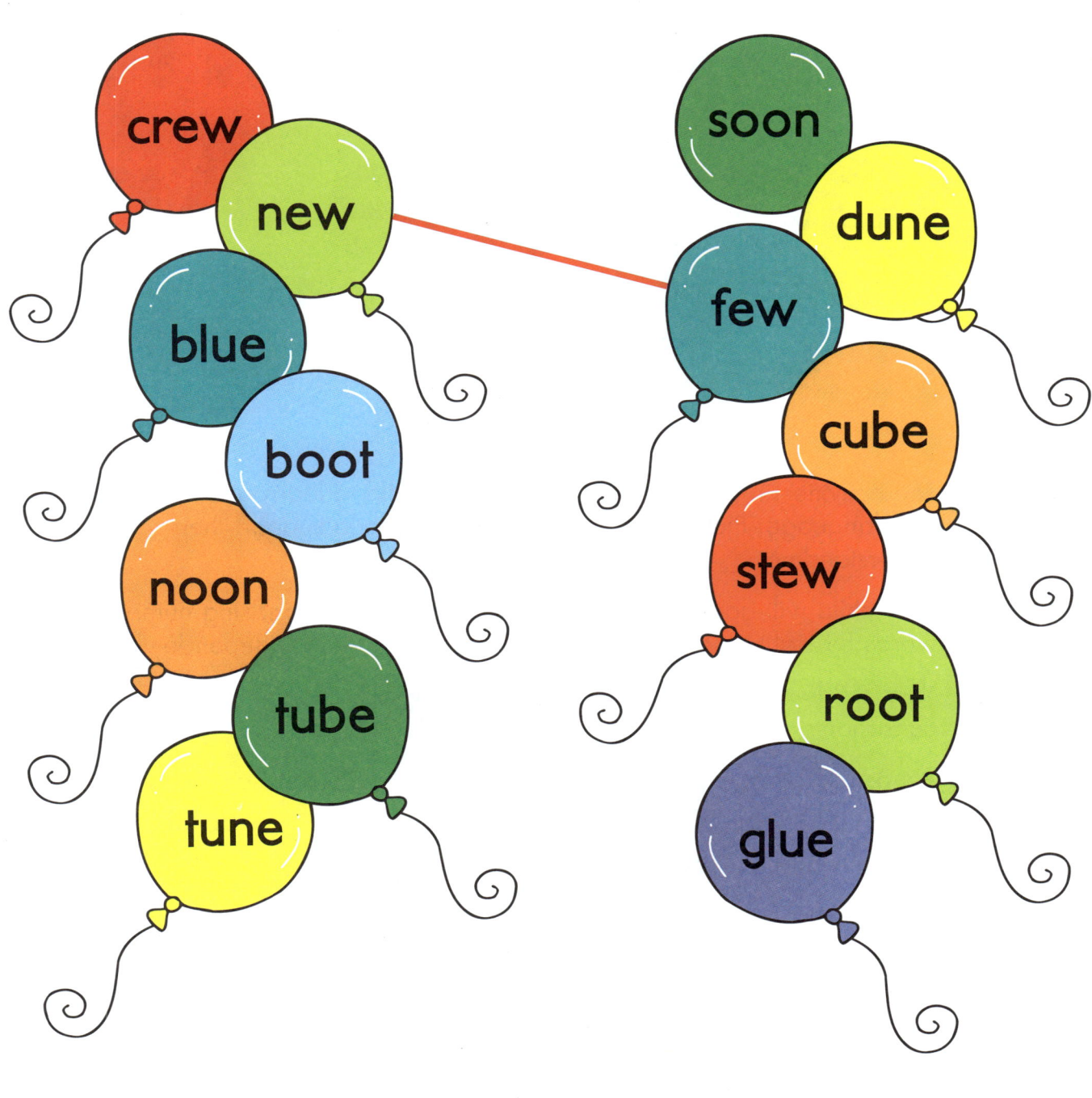

Reading and Language Arts

Helping Your Child

- The activities in this section will help your child to learn about reading and language. Pictures provide hints and clues to support their understanding.

- Your child will gain the confidence to: identify an increasing number of words by sight, spell new words, and begin to read independently.

- Your child will learn about: common sight words, beginning and end consonants, and plurals.

- Set aside time to do the activities together. Do a little at a time so that your child enjoys learning.

- Give lots of encouragement and praise.

- The answers are on pages 124—125.

Contents

All about Me	38
Yes or No?	39
The Enormous Turnip	40
How Does It End?	41
Read and Draw	42
Making Sentences	43
Animal Dictionary	44
Reading an Index	45
Days of the Week	46
Useful Words	47
Introducing Syllables	48
Clap Our Names	49
Syllables	50
How Many Syllables?	51
More Than One	52
Quick Quiz	53
Plurals	54
Words Ending in -er or -est	55
Read a Story	56
Read a Poem	58
Sight Test 1	59
Read Nonfiction	60
Read a Fairy Tale	62
Sight Words	64
More Sight Words	65

All about Me

Write in the missing words.

My name is ………………………………………….

I am ……………… years old.

I live at ……………………………………………

………………………………………………………

……………………………………………………….

My school is called …………………………………….

My favorite animal is ……………………….

My favorite sport is …………………………………….

Yes or No?

Look at the picture. Read the sentences and write **yes** or **no** next to each one.

The teacher is under the table. ....
The girl is reading a book. ....
The boy is painting the door. ....
The teacher is looking at the girl. ....
The cat is reading a book. ....
The boy has a brush. ....
The hamster is on its cage. ....

The Enormous Turnip

Look at the pictures. Read the sentences.
Connect each sentence to the correct picture.

Everyone fell over and the turnip came out. ....

The farmer saw an enormous turnip. ....

Everyone tried to pull up the turnip. ....

The farmer tried to pull up the turnip. ....

Note for parent: This activity gives your child practice in sequencing and making sense of a simple story.

How Does It End?

Look at each row of pictures. Tell the story but choose the ending that you like the best.

Note for parent: This activity gives your child experience telling a simple story in their own words, making sense of pictures, and placing events in a logical order.

Read and Draw

Read the sentences and finish the picture.

Draw a tree <u>by</u> the river.
Draw a boat going <u>under</u> the bridge.
Draw a duck <u>on</u> the river.
Draw a car going <u>over</u> the bridge.
Draw a sun <u>up</u> in the sky.

Note for parent: This activity helps children to learn positional words such as by, under, on, over, and up.

Making Sentences

These sentences are all muddled. Write the words in the right order and then finish each one with a period (.) or a question mark (?).

is time What it

....

fruit I to like eat

....

do go school When I to

....

car going The was fast

....

up Who the with went Jill hill

....

on lap The likes sit to my cat

....

How many capital letters can you count? ....

Animal Dictionary

Draw a line to connect each word to the correct meaning.

 **elephant**

A large animal that can jump very well. It carries its young in a pouch. It comes from Australia.

 **kangaroo**

A small animal with long arms and feet that it uses like hands. It lives in jungles.

monkey

A large animal with a long trunk and ivory tusks. It lives in Africa and Asia.

panda

An animal like a horse with black and white stripes. It lives in Africa.

zebra

A black and white animal that lives in China.

Reading an Index

Use the index below to answer the questions at the bottom of the page.

Index

Apes	10	Kangaroos	20
Bears	8	Monkeys	6
Chimpanzees	14	Penguins	28
Crocodiles	22	Sharks	4
Dolphins	26	Turtles	12
Giraffes	18	Whales	16

Page 18 is about ....

Page 28 is about ....

Page 16 is about ....

Page 8 is about ....

Page 12 is about ....

Apes are on page ....

Sharks are on page ....

Kangaroos are on page ....

Giraffes are on page ....

Chimpanzees are on page ....

Which page would you like to read? ....

Why? ....

....

Note for parent: Using an index is an important skill for your child to learn.

Days of the Week

Clare

Jack

Look at the pictures. Read the questions and then write the correct day. Remember the capital letters.

Monday

When does Clare go trampolining? ....

When does Clare watch TV? ....

Tuesday

When does Jack go to the library? ....

When does Clare go grocery shopping? ....

Wednesday

When does Jack wash the car? ....

When does Clare take the dog out? ....

Thursday

When does Jack play soccer? ....

Friday

Saturday

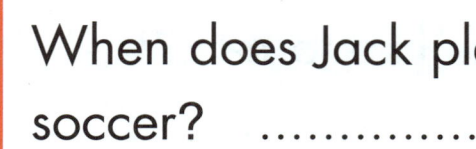
Sunday

Note for parent: This activity helps your child to use their comprehension skills, as well as learn to write the days of the week.

Useful Words

Some words are not easy to read by blending the sounds of the letters. You need to learn these words by heart. See if you can remember these useful words.

the	said	once	she
you	was	they	
are	come	his	time

Can you spot any of these words in the story below? Draw a circle around each word in the story.

Once upon a time there lived a king.

He was very sad. He had lost his crown.

The queen was kind.

She said: "You are OK. Come on—let's look for it."

They found it in the garden.

Note for parent: Explain to your child that there are some words that we can't sound out (decode).

Introducing Syllables

Count the syllables (or beats) in these words as you sound them out.

For example: **dog** has one syllable.
el/e/phant has three.

Draw lines in the words to separate the syllables.

- umbrella
- snowman
- spider
- mug
- jellyfish
- wardrobe
- holiday
- octopus

Note for parent: Use the word beat instead of syllable, if you prefer, and clap the beats in each word as you sound it out.

Clap Our Names

Read the names on the school register. Clap the syllables in each name.

For example: **Cin/de/rell/a** has four beats!

Ali

Ella

Isabella

Jim

Katya

Mohammad

Nazeem

Oliver

Poppy

Harry

Note for parent: Try your child's name first. Do you know any longer names? Rumpelstiltskin has four beats!

Syllables

A syllable is the part of a word that sounds like a beat as we say the word. Try reading these words.

ca-mel	di-no-saur	ro-bot
rab-bit	ba-na-na	car-rot

Read the sentences below. Look at the picture and write the correct word to complete each sentence.

The book was about a ....
camel / dinosaur

 The .... was big and blue.
rabbit / robot

The rabbit ate a ....
banana / carrot

Note for parent: Clap as you say each syllable. See if your child can count how many syllables there are in each word.

How Many Syllables?

Look at the words below. Count how many syllables are in each word. Write the numbers in the boxes.

January		July	
February		August	
March		September	
April		October	
May		November	
June		December	

Note for parent: Encourage your child to clap the beat for each syllable as they sound out each word.

More Than One

You add the letter **s** when there is more than one. Write the whole words in the spaces.

duck　　_ _ _ _ _

pig　　_ _ _ _

cow　　_ _ _ _

farmer　　_ _ _ _ _ _ _

cat　　_ _ _ _

Quick Quiz

What are these sentences describing?

Choose a word to write at the end of each one.

1. This sails across the sea.   _ _ _ _

2. You find this on a farm.   _ _ _ _ _

3. You find this on the beach.   _ _ _ _ _

Add the letter **s** when there is more than one. Write the whole words in the spaces.

Note for parent: This is a quick revision of some of the learning covered so far.

Plurals

Plural means more than one. To make the plural, we add an **s**. Write the plural for each of these words on the lines. The first one has been done for you.

singular		plural
book		books
chair		
lamp		
pencil		
sock		

Note for parent: Explain to your child the simplest way to form plurals is to add **s** to the end of a word.

Words Ending in -er or -est

Read the words in the boxes. Choose the correct word to match each picture. Write the word on the line.

big

bigger

biggest

....big........   ....

tall

taller

tallest

..tallest....   ....

Note for parent: Help your child to think of some other words that have -er and -est endings. For example: long, longer, longest and strong, stronger, strongest.

Read a Story

Read the story below.

Bella's Bedtime

It was Bella's bedtime, but she couldn't find Bertie Bear, and she didn't want to go to sleep without him.

She looked on the bedroom floor, in the toy box, and under the bed.

"I'm sure we'll find him tomorrow," said Mom.

Bella wiped away her tears and pulled back the blanket.

Bertie was fast asleep on her pillow!

Read the sentences below. Choose the correct word to complete each sentence. Draw a circle around each correct answer.

At the beginning of the story, Bella couldn't find …

 her shoes / Bertie Bear

Bella looked for Bertie Bear in the …

 bedroom / bathroom

Mom said that they would …

buy another bear / find him tomorrow

Note for parent: Encourage your child to look back at the story to find the answers in the text. Talking about what happened will extend your child's comprehension skills.

Read a Poem

Read the poem below. Find the rhyming words at the end of the lines. Trace over each pair of rhyming words with the same-colored pencil.

Twinkle, Twinkle, Little Star

Twinkle, twinkle, little star,

How I wonder what you are!

Up above the world so high,

Like a diamond in the sky.

When the blazing sun is gone,

When it nothing shines upon,

Then you show your little light,

Twinkle, twinkle, all the night.

Note for parent: Enjoy reading the poem together. Try reading it in different ways. For example: in a whisper, very slowly, and exaggerating the rhyming words.

Sight Test 1

Which is correct? Circle the correct word.

- sed or **said**
- **some** or som
- hav or **have**
- littel or **little**
- soe or **so**
- com or **come**
- **like** or lyke
- **there** or thare

Note for parent: This activity will help your child to recognize common sight words.

Read Nonfiction

Read about Zac and Zoe.

Zac and Zoe are twins. Although they are twins, they like different things.

Zac

Zoe

Zac likes science and Zoe likes math.

Zac likes tennis and Zoe likes soccer.

Zac and Zoe both like reading.

Note for parent: This activity encourages your child to read for meaning and find answers in a text, which will help to increase comprehension skills.

Answer these questions about Zac and Zoe.
Write the correct names on the lines.

Who likes tennis? ....

Who likes math? ....

Who likes science? ....

Who likes soccer? ....

Choose one present for Zac and Zoe to share. What would they both like? Draw a circle around the object.

tennis racket

soccer ball

book

Read a Fairy Tale

Read this passage from a traditional fairy tale.

Goldilocks and the Three Bears

Goldilocks tasted the porridge in the big bowl.

"This porridge is too salty," she said.

Then Goldilocks tasted the porridge in the medium bowl.

"This porridge is too sweet," she said.

Finally, Goldilocks tasted the porridge in the small bowl.

"Yummy! This porridge is just right," she said, and ate it all up.

Read the sentences in the boxes below. Choose the correct word to complete each sentence.
Write the words on the lines.

| big | medium | small |

The porridge in the ……………… bowl was too sweet.

The porridge in the ……………… bowl was too salty.

The porridge in the ……………… bowl was just right.

Retell the passage in your own words.

………………………………………………………………………
………………………………………………………………………
………………………………………………………………………
………………………………………………………………………
………………………………………………………………………

Sight Words

Read and try to remember what these sight words look like.

Note for parent: There is no easy way of learning these words. But with practice and familiarity, your child will begin to recognize them on sight.

More Sight Words

Read and try to remember what these tricky sight words look like.

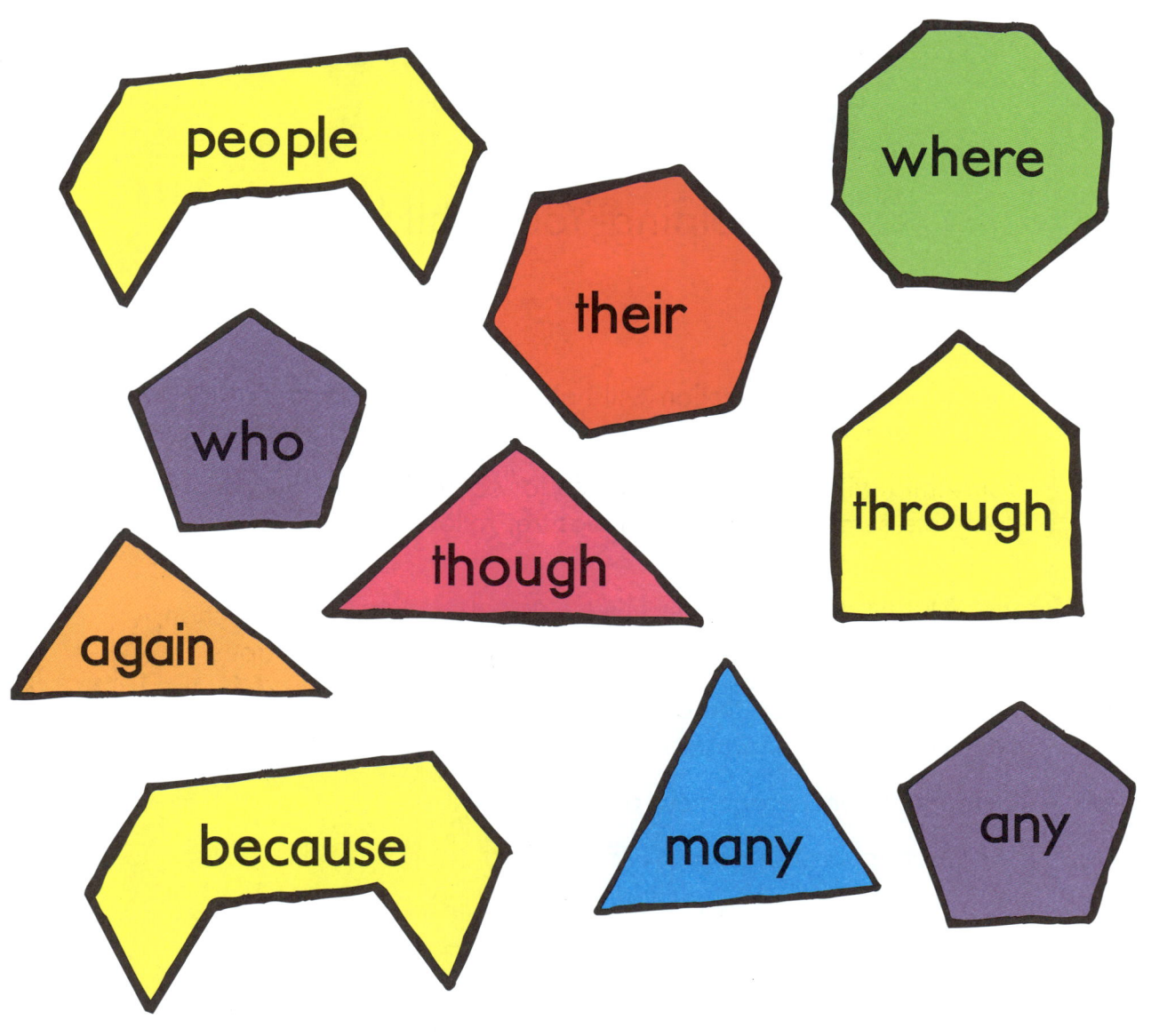

Note for parent: There is no easy way of learning these words. But with practice and familiarity your child will begin to recognize them on sight.

Math

Helping Your Child

- The activities in this section will help your child learn about math. Pictures provide hints and clues to support their understanding.

- Your child will gain the confidence to: count forward and backward, complete sums, estimate and measure, follow instructions, and solve problems.

- Your child will learn about: number bonds, addition, subtraction, multiplication, division, fractions, measurements, and shapes.

- Set aside time to do the activities together. Do a little at a time so that your child enjoys learning.

- Give lots of encouragement and praise.

- The answers are on pages 125—127.

Contents

Counting to 10	68
Counting to 15	69
Number Words 1 to 20	70
What's Missing?	72
Counting On	74
Counting Back	75
Numbers to 30	76
Counting to 50	77
Two-Way Counts	78
Adding More	79
Counting in Tens	80
Addition	82
Taking Away	84
Making 20	86
Number Bonds to 20	87
Addition Facts	88
Subtraction Facts	89
Counting up to 100	90
Number Lines	91
Tens and Ones to 50	92
Ordering Numbers	94
Missing Numbers	95

Counting to 10

Count all the apples and write the number in the box. Use the number line to help you.

apples

1 2 3 4 5 6 7 8 9 10

Counting to 15

Count the balls and write the total number in the box.

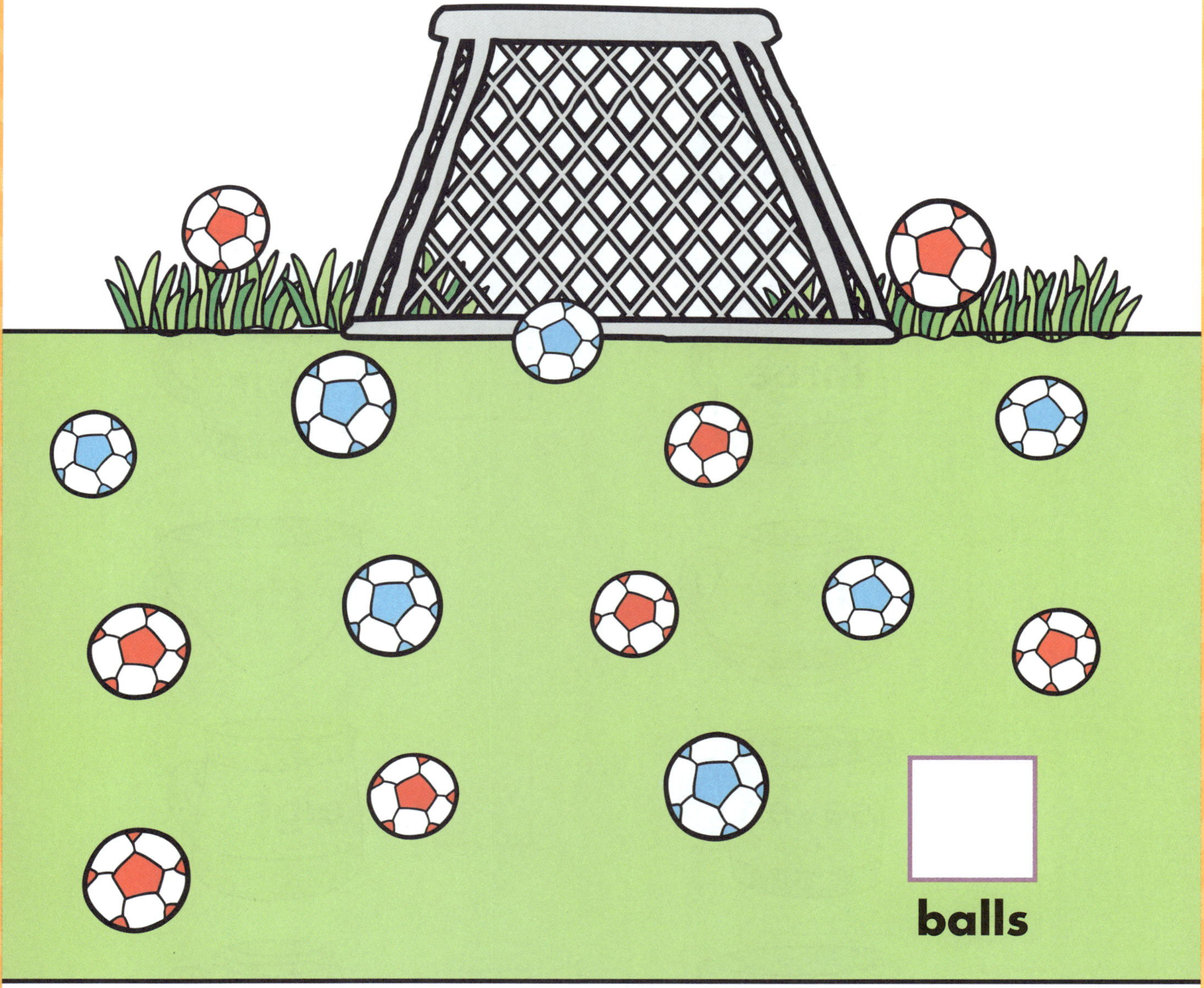

balls

11 12 13 14 15

Note for parent: Encourage your child to write the number clearly and neatly.

Number Words 1 to 20

Write the correct number next to each word to count from one to twenty.

What's Missing?

Write the missing numbers in each sequence.

Counting On

Count on from these numbers. Use the number line to help you. Write the answer in the box.

Count on 4 from 3 ☐

Count on 5 from 6 ☐

Count on 7 from 9 ☐

Count on 10 from 4 ☐

Count on 11 from 8 ☐

Count on 11 from 2 ☐

Note for parent: These activities reinforce counting forward in ones to 20 using a number line.

Counting Back

Count back from these numbers. Use the number line to help you. Write the answer in the box.

Count back 5 from 12 ☐

Count back 6 from 17 ☐

Count back 8 from 18 ☐

Count back 14 from 20 ☐

Count back 12 from 20 ☐

Count back 3 from 19 ☐

1 2 3 4 5 6 7 8 9 10

11 12 13 14 15 16 17 18 19 20

Note for parent: These activities reinforce counting backward in ones from 20 using a number line.

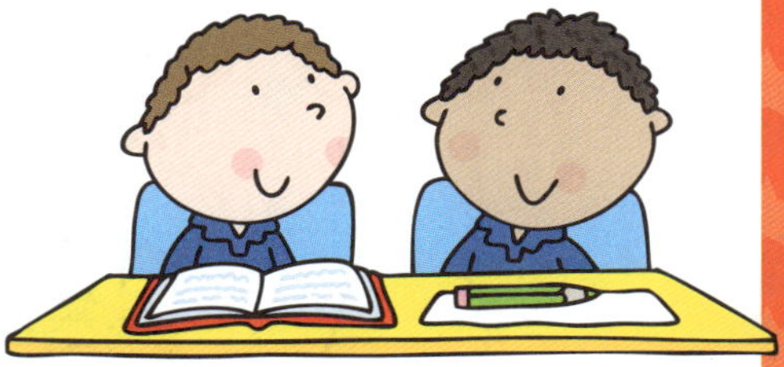

Numbers to 30

Fill in the missing numbers in the balloons.

Counting to 50

Try counting the blocks in this box. Write the total.

blocks

Now try counting the blocks in this box. Write the total.

blocks

When you need to count a big number of items, try putting them in groups or columns.

Note for parent: Try counting objects found around your home using this method.

Two-Way Counts

Count back one less and count on one more than each of the numbers shown. Write the answers in the boxes.

Adding More

Write the number that is two more each time.

Write the number that is two more each time.

Note for parent: This activity prepares your child for adding and subtracting.

Counting in Tens

Count forward in tens. Write the missing numbers in each row. Use the number line to help you.

Count backward in tens. Write the missing numbers in each row. Use the number line to help you.

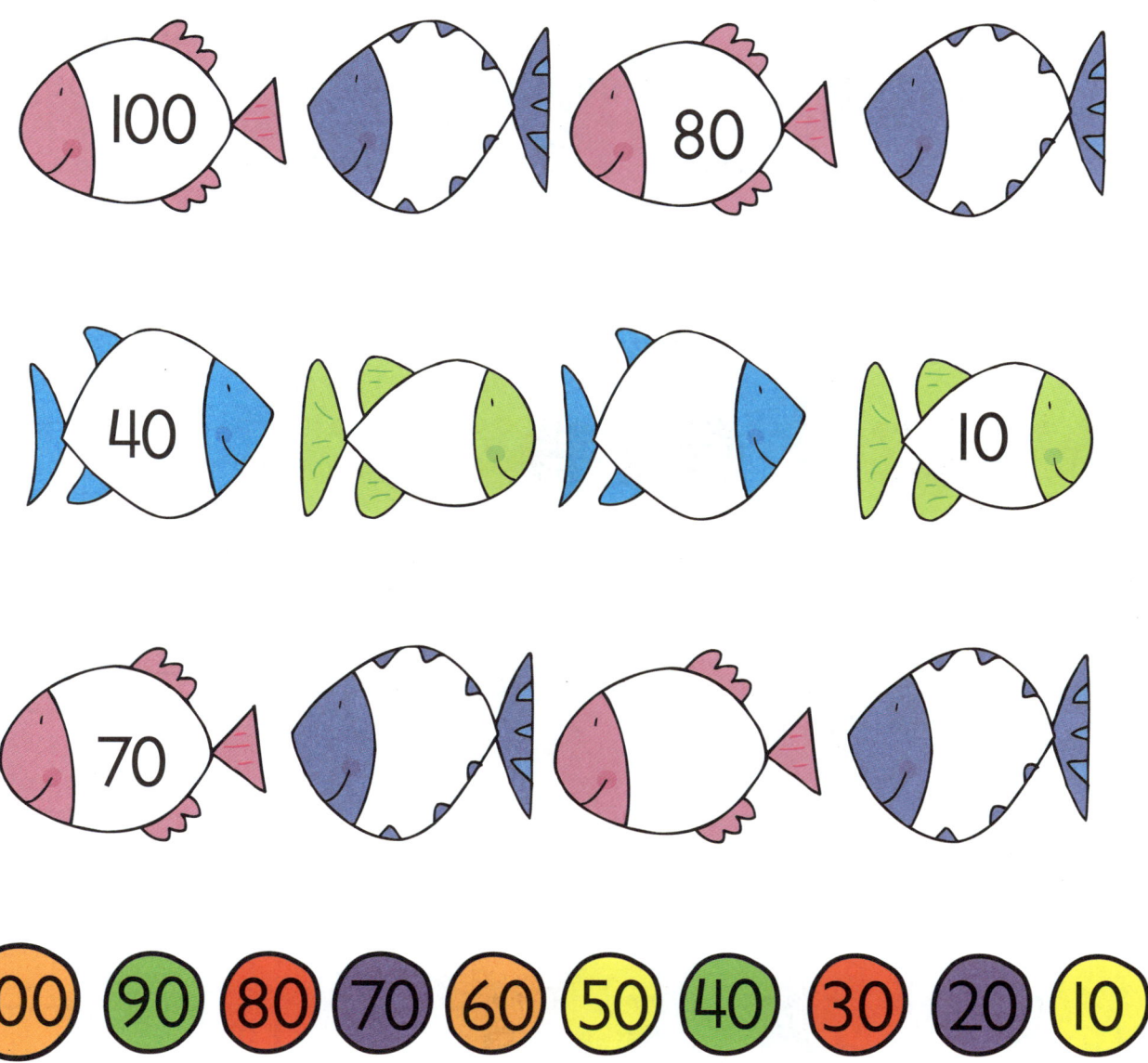

Addition

+ is the addition or plus sign

two ladybugs plus three ladybugs = five ladybugs

2 + 3 = 5

Addition can be done in any order. Work out these addition sums.

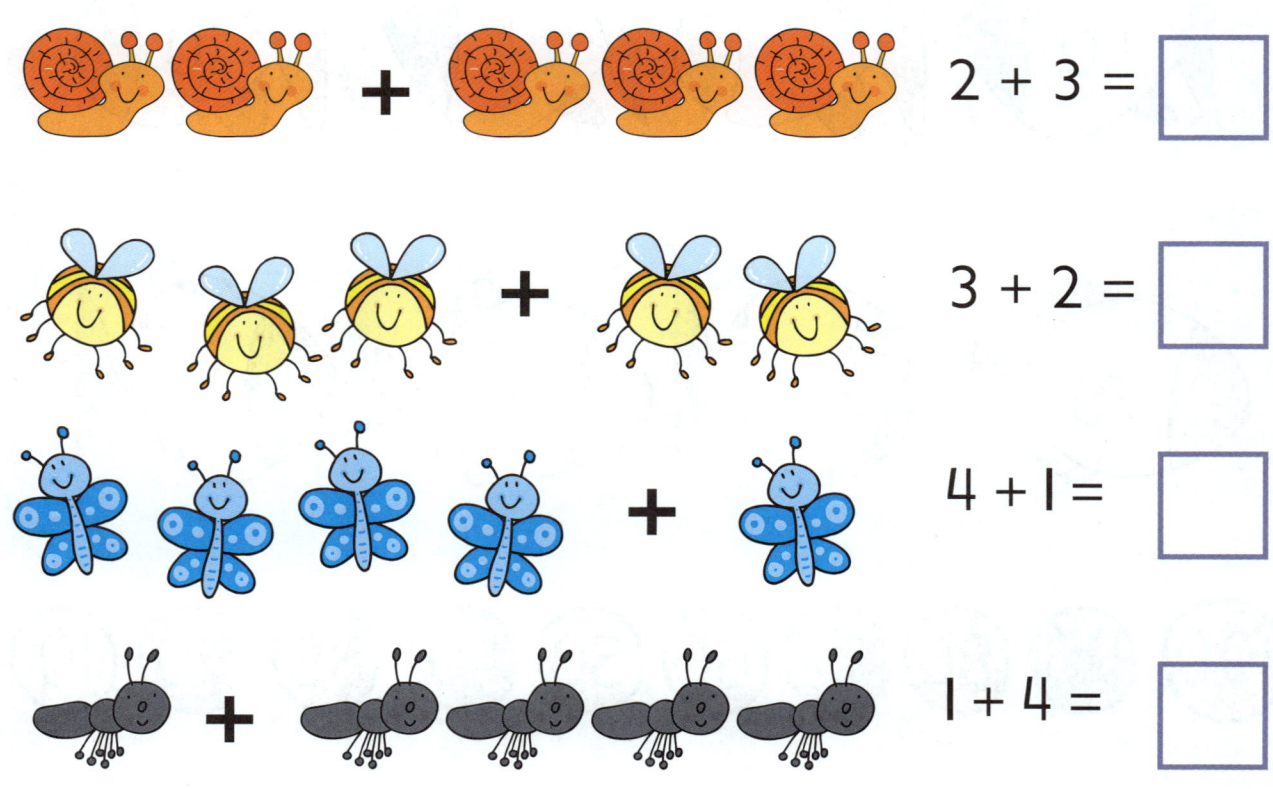

2 + 3 =

3 + 2 =

4 + 1 =

1 + 4 =

Note for parent: This activity demonstrates that addition can be done in any order and that different number pairs can equal the same sum.

Answer these addition sums. Put the answers in the box. Use the number line to help you.

5 add 1

What is the sum of 2 and 6?

What must I add to 3 to make 10?

6 plus 2

What is the total of 3 and 6?

How many are 3 and 5 altogether?

Add 3 to 4

Note for parent: This activity introduces your child to the different vocabulary that can be used for addition sums.

Taking Away

– is the take away or minus sign

Cross off the treats to be taken away. Write how many are left.

 take away 3   5 – 3 = ☐

 take away 2   5 – 2 = ☐

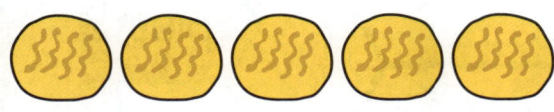 take away 4   5 – 4 = ☐

 take away 1   5 – 1 = ☐

 take away 0   5 – 0 = ☐

Write the answer to these sums in the boxes.
Use the number line to help you.

4 take away 2 = ☐

Take 2 from 7 = ☐

7 subtract 3 = ☐

Subtract 2 from 10 = ☐

8 less than 9 = ☐

What is the difference between 3 and 9? ☐

How many less than 6 is 4? ☐

I think of a number. I take away 3. My answer is 7.
What is my number? ☐

Making 20

Count the beads on each string. Draw and color in more beads to make 20 on each string. Write how many extra beads you have to draw in the box.

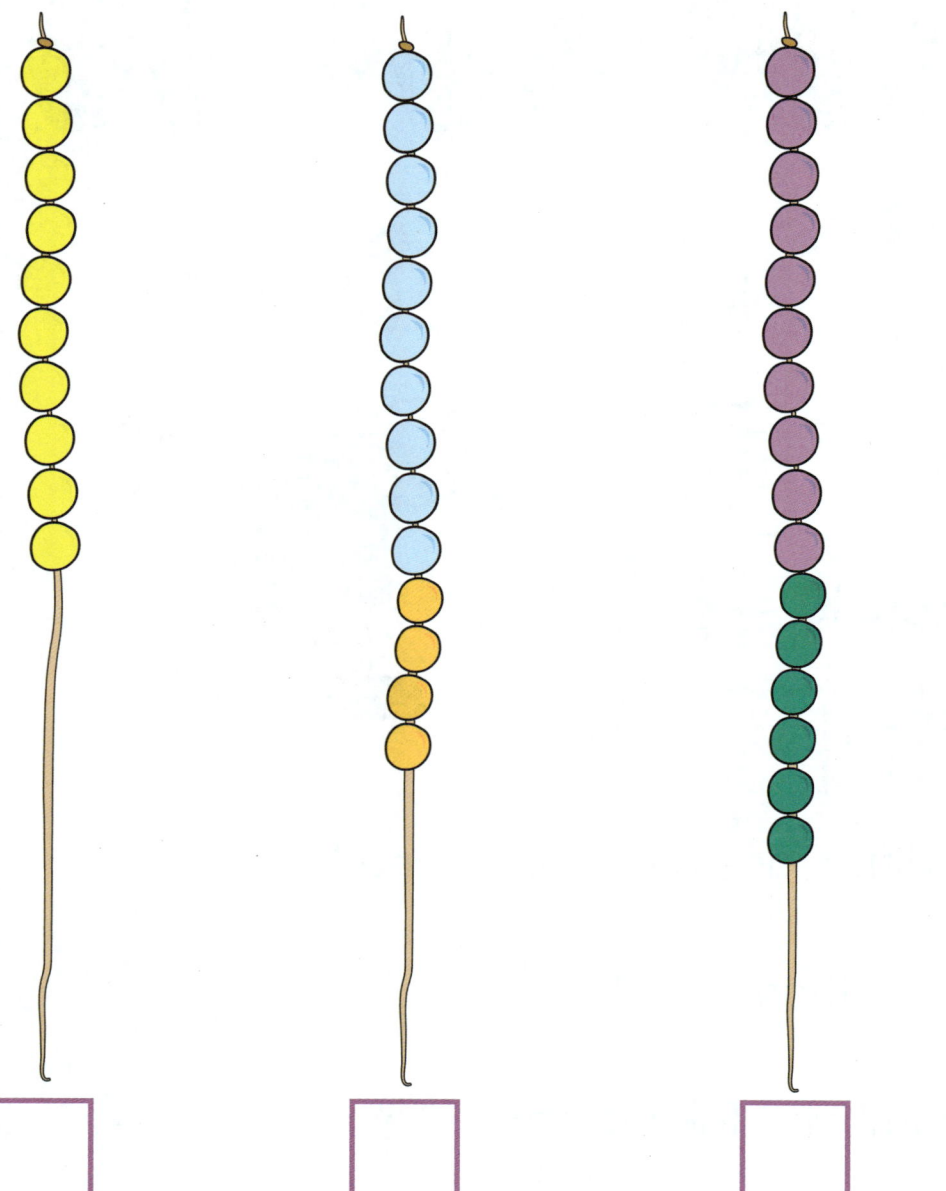

Number Bonds to 20

Draw a line to match a moon and a star to make a total of 20.

Note for parent: This activity demonstrates how different pairs added together can make the same number.

Addition Facts

Different pairs added together can add up to the same number. Work out these addition number bonds to 10.

0 + ☐ = 10      10 + ☐ = 10

1 + 9 = ☐   ☐ + 1 = 10

☐ + 8 = 10   ☐ + 2 = 10

3 + ☐ = 10   7 + 3 = ☐

4 + 6 = ☐   6 + ☐ = 10

☐ + 5 = 10   5 + ☐ = 10

Note for parent: Explain to your child that for addition pairs it does not matter in what order they are added together.

Subtraction Facts

Work out these subtraction number bonds to 10.

$10 - 0 = \square$ $10 - 10 = \square$

$\square - 1 = 9$ $10 - \square = 1$

$10 - \square = 8$ $\square - 8 = \square$

$10 - 3 = \square$ $10 - \square = 3$

$\square - 4 = \square$ $10 - 6 = \square$

$10 - \square = 5$ $10 - 5 = \square$

Note for parent: Familiarity with different number bonds will help your child with number operations like subtraction.

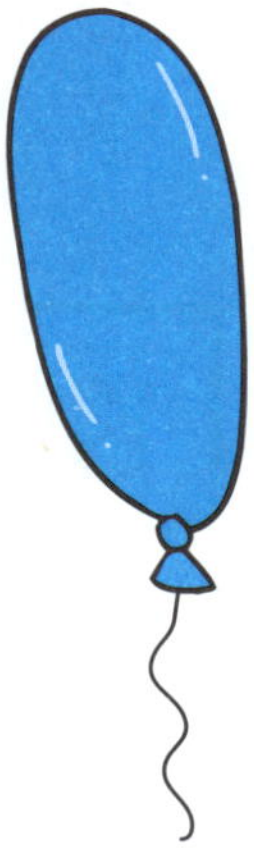

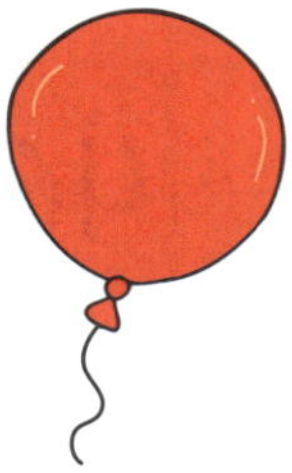

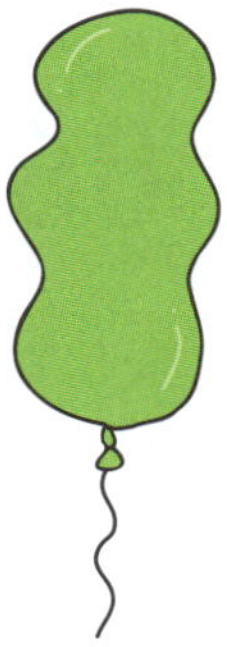

Counting up to 100

Fill in the missing numbers up to 100. When you have completed the table, try counting backward from 100 to 1.

1	2	3	4	5	6	7		9	
11		13		15		17			20
	22	23			26	27			30
31	32		34	35			38		
41			44		46		48		50
	52	53		55		57			60
61			64		66		68		
	72			75				79	80
81		83			86		88		
	92		94			97		99	

Note for parent: Have fun counting backward together by taking turns to say a number each.

Number Lines

Count forward and backward in tens using the number lines. Write the next numbers in the sequence.

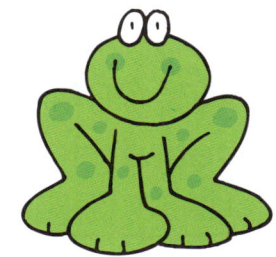

10	20	30	40	50					

100	90	80	70	60					

11	21	31	41	51					

93	83	73	63	53					

Note for parent: This activity gives practice in counting forward and backward in tens.

Tens and Ones to 50

How many groups of ten are in each group? How many ones are in each group? Add the numbers together to find the total number in each group.

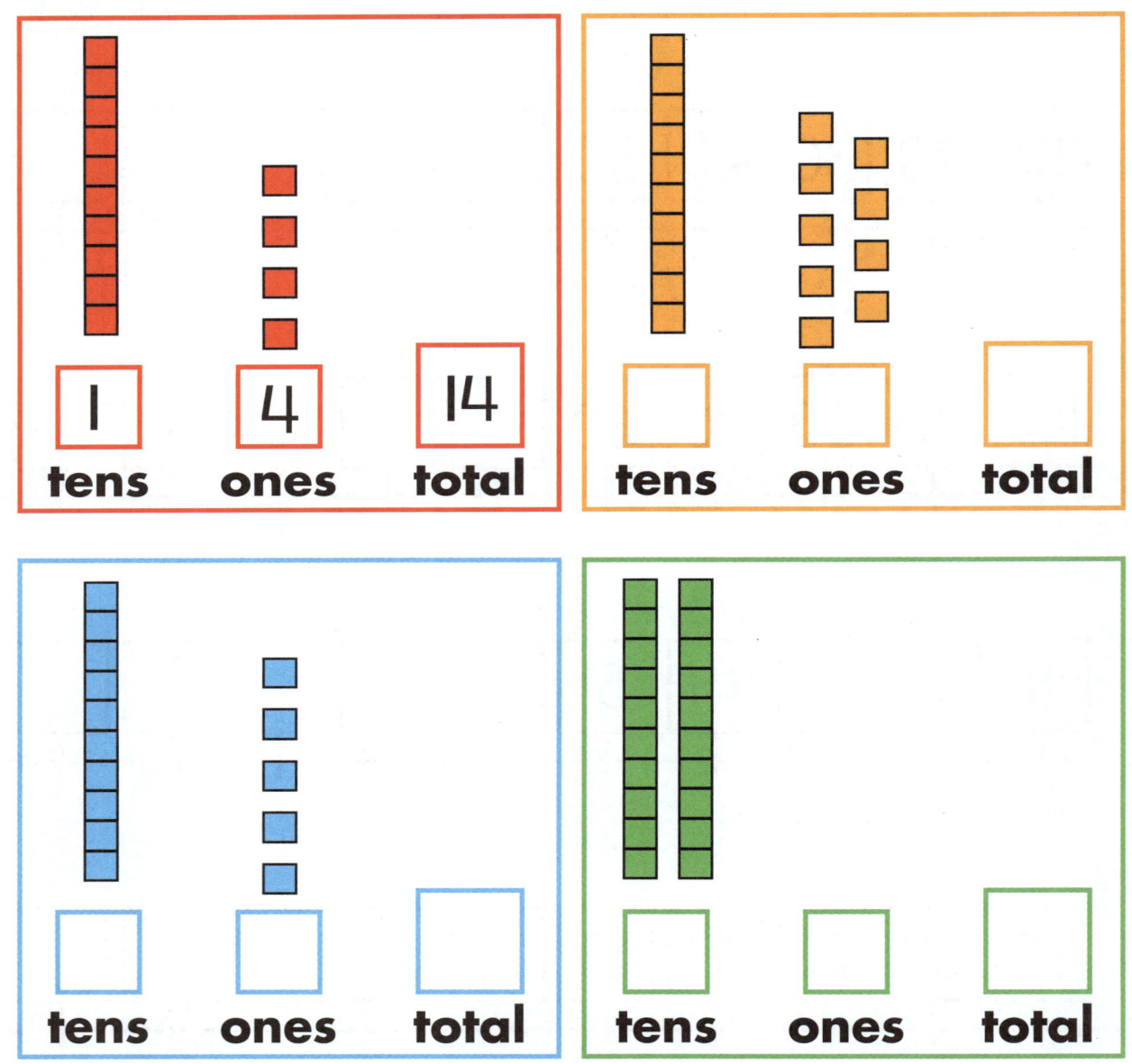

How many groups of ten are in each group?
How many ones are in each group?
Add the numbers together to find the total number of squares in each group.

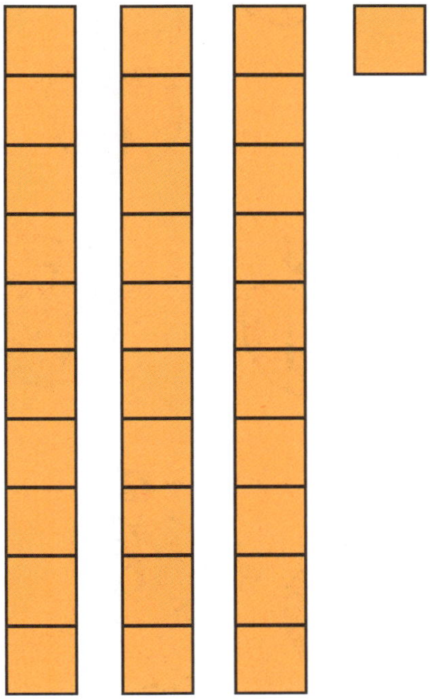

tens ones

total

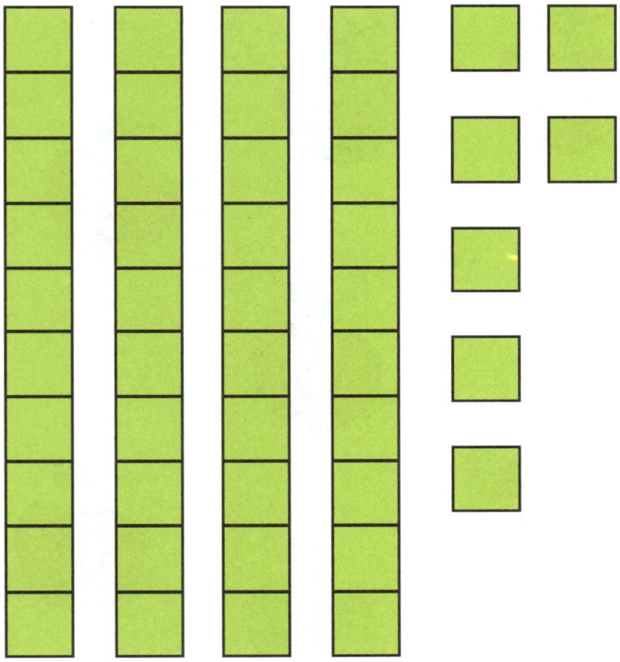

tens ones

total

Note for parent: Sound out the additions for your child. Say: 3 groups of ten and 1 equals 31 all together.

Ordering Numbers

Draw an arrow from one apple to another, placing them in the correct number order to 30.

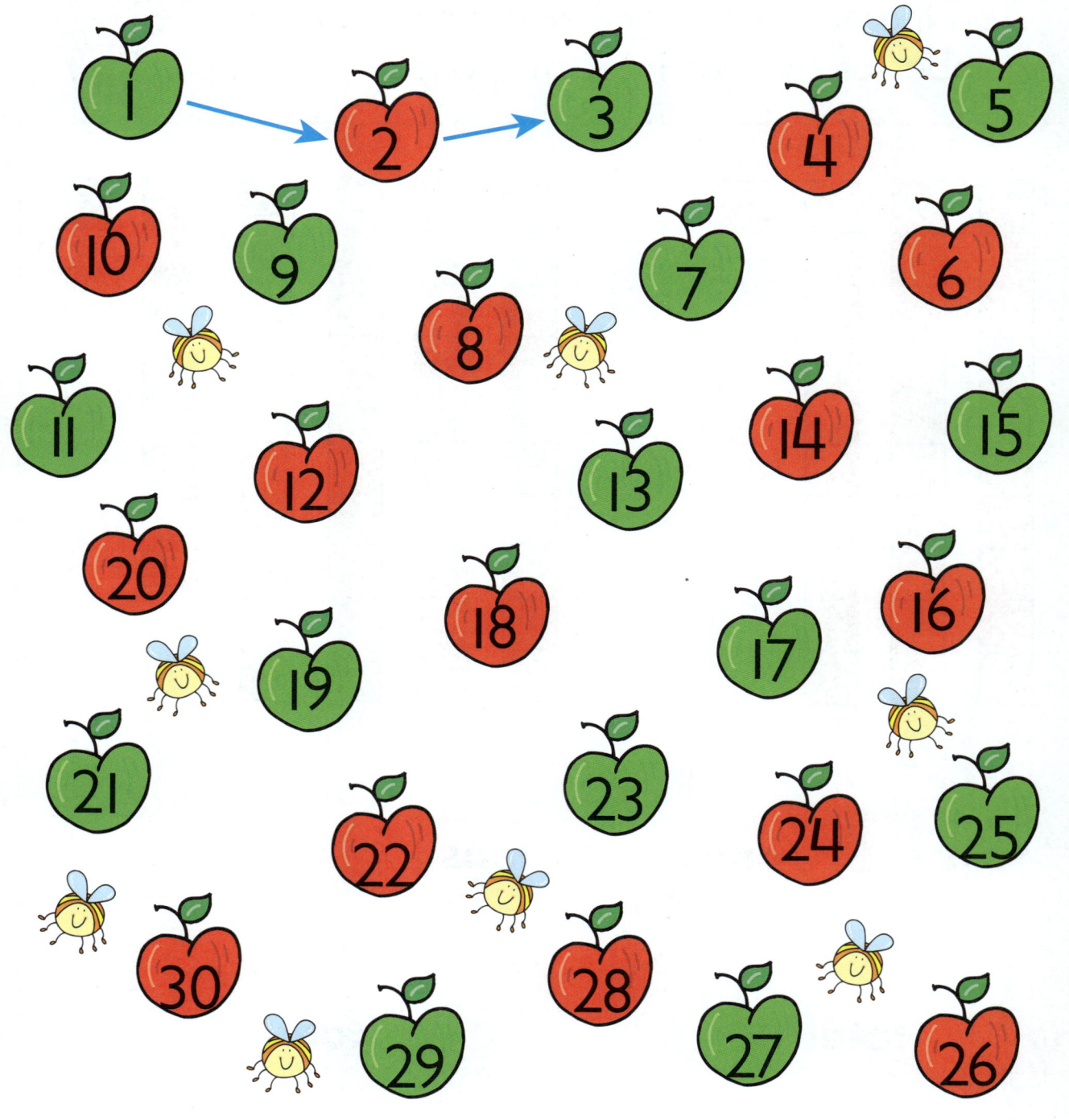

Missing Numbers

Count the bananas in number order and fill in the missing numbers. Write the total number of bananas.

Space, Measurement, and Time

Helping Your Child

- The activities in this section will help your child to learn about space, measurement and time. Pictures provide hints and clues to support their understanding.

- Your child will gain the confidence to: use a range of measures to describe and compare different quantities such as length, mass, capacity, and volume.

- Your child will learn about: units of time, how we measure and record numerical information, and 2D and 3D shapes.

- Set aside time to do the activities together. Do a little at a time so that your child enjoys learning.

- Give lots of encouragement and praise.

- The answers are on pages 127– 128.

Contents

How Long?	98
How Heavy?	100
How Much?	102
2D Shapes	104
Sorting Shapes	105
Counting Shapes	106
3D Shapes	108
Directions	110
Telling the Time	112
Temperature	114
Match the Shape	116
Draw Shapes	117
Properties of 2D Shapes	118
Properties of 3D Shapes	120
Tally Charts	122

How Long?

Use a ruler to measure the length of each object in centimeters. Write the answer in the box.

☐ cm

☐ cm

☐ cm

☐ cm

True or false? Check your answer.
The fish is the shortest object.
The watch is the longest object.

true **false**
☐ ☐
☐ ☐

Note for parent: This activity gives your child practice measuring. Try measuring other objects around your home.

Use a ruler to measure the length of each of these objects in inches. Write the answers in the table.

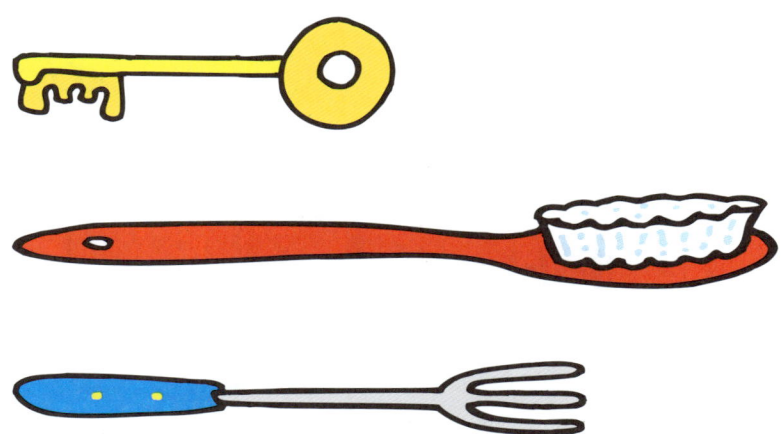

object	inches
key	
toothbrush	
fork	

Draw an object that measures 4 cm or 1.5 in.

How Heavy?

Draw a circle around the word that best describes the weight of these objects.

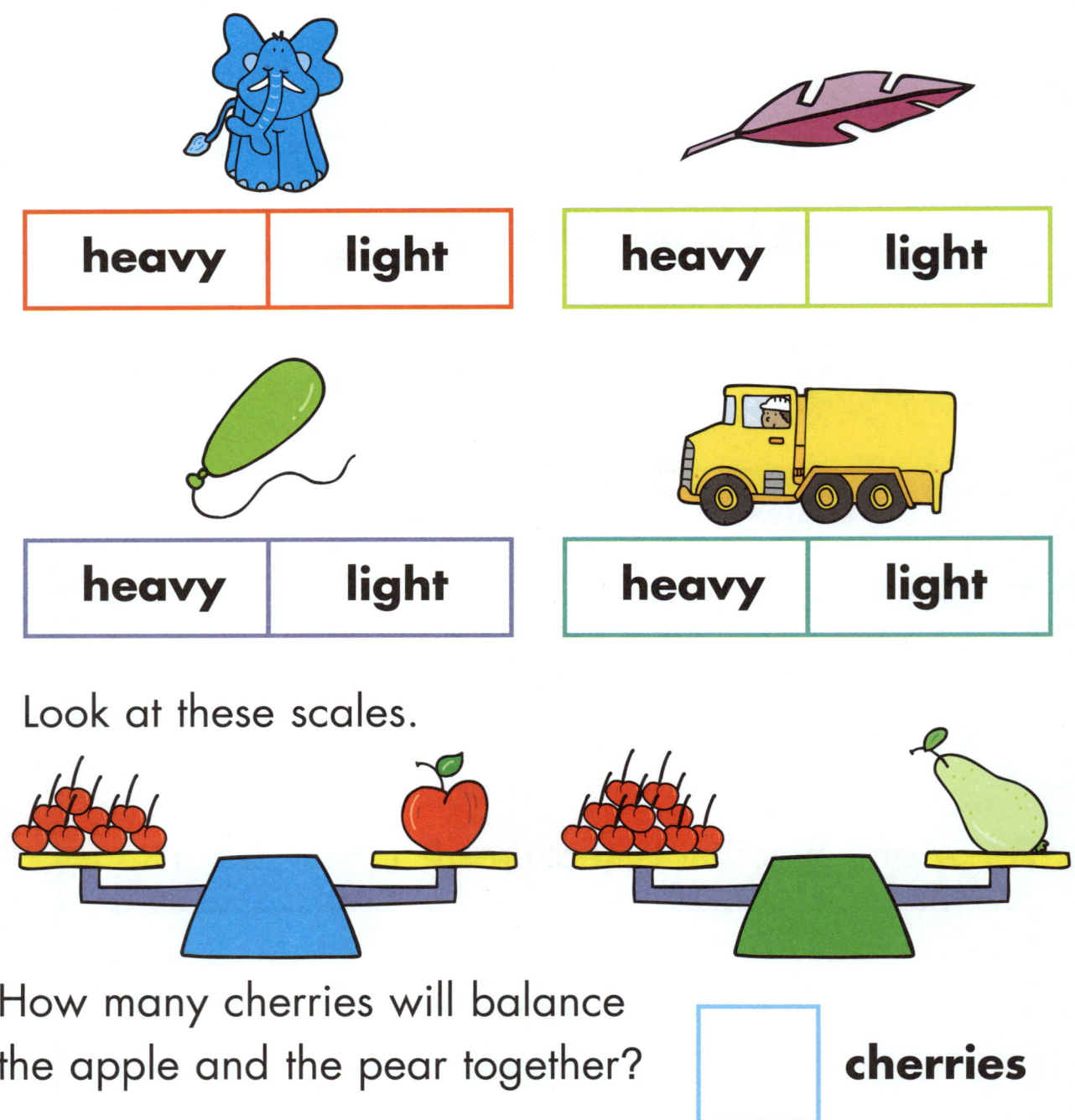

Look at these scales.

How many cherries will balance the apple and the pear together? ☐ **cherries**

To find the weight of each object on the weighing scale, count the numbers from 0. Write the answer in the box. Weights can be grams, ounces, pounds, and more.

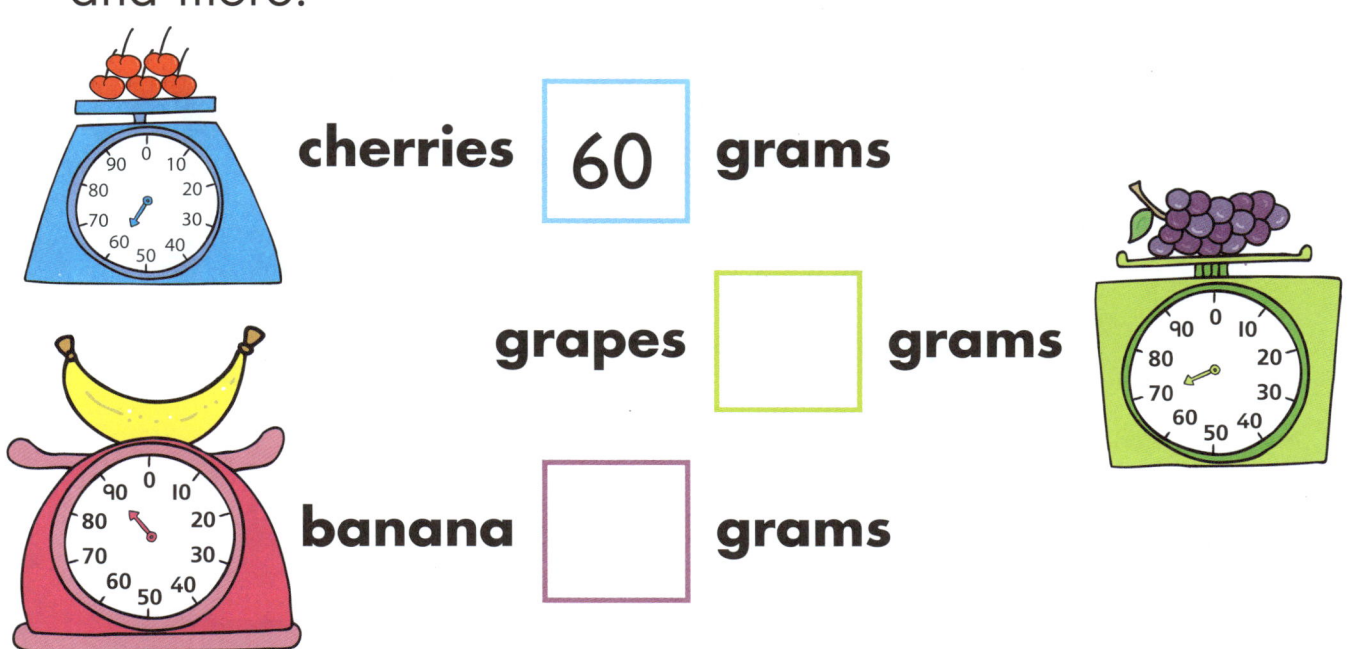

cherries 60 grams

grapes ☐ grams

banana ☐ grams

Read these sentences. Draw a circle around the words to make each statement correct.

The cherries are **heavier than / lighter than** the grapes.

The banana is **heavier than / lighter than** the cherries.

The grapes are **heavier than / lighter than** the banana.

Note for parent: This activity helps your child to recognize how numbers are useful in everyday life.

How Much?

Liquid can be measured in ounces, gallons, liters, and more. How much water is in each of the jugs?

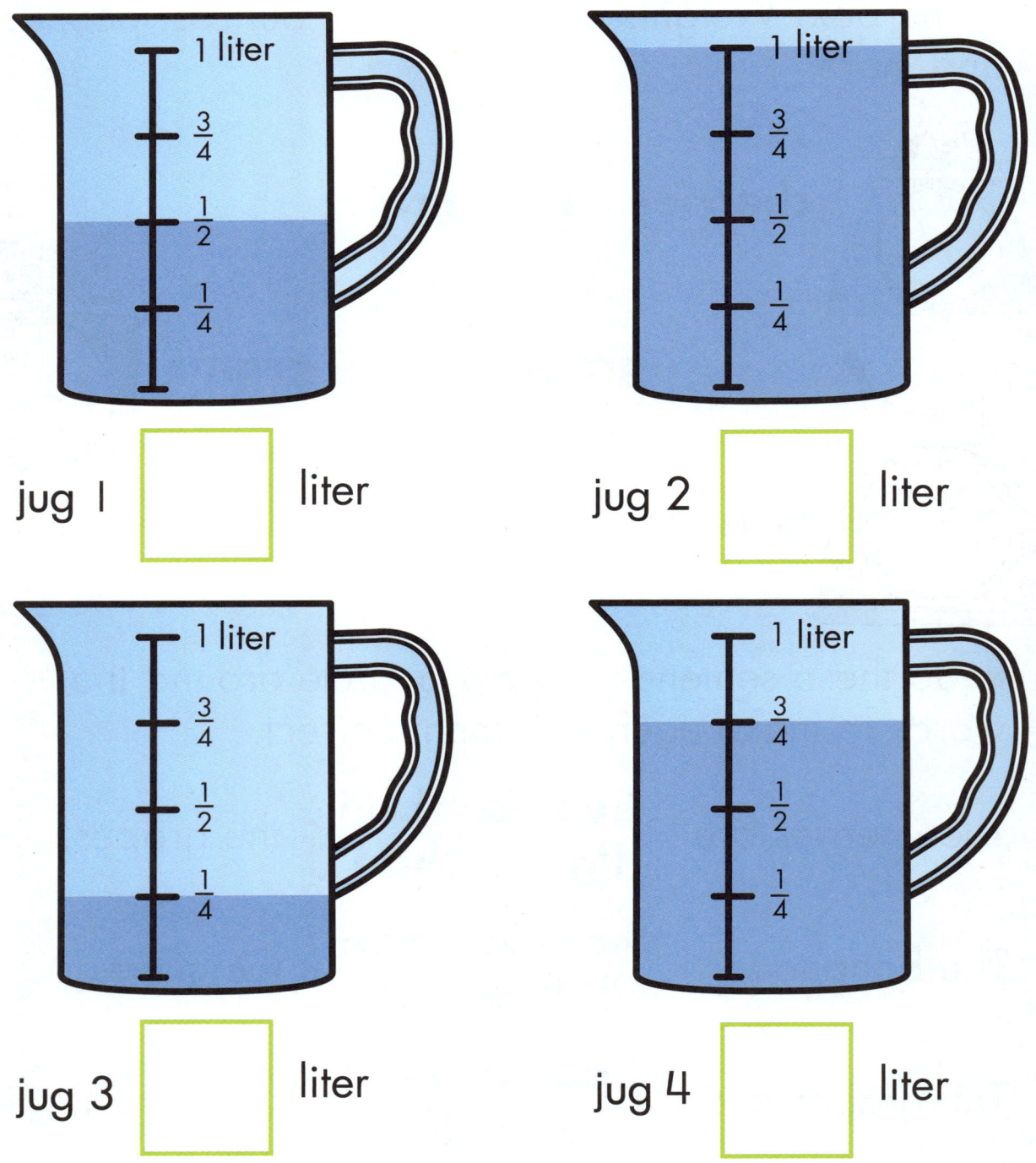

jug 1 [ ] liter

jug 2 [ ] liter

jug 3 [ ] liter

jug 4 [ ] liter

Look at how many milliliters (ml) of water there is in each of these jugs.

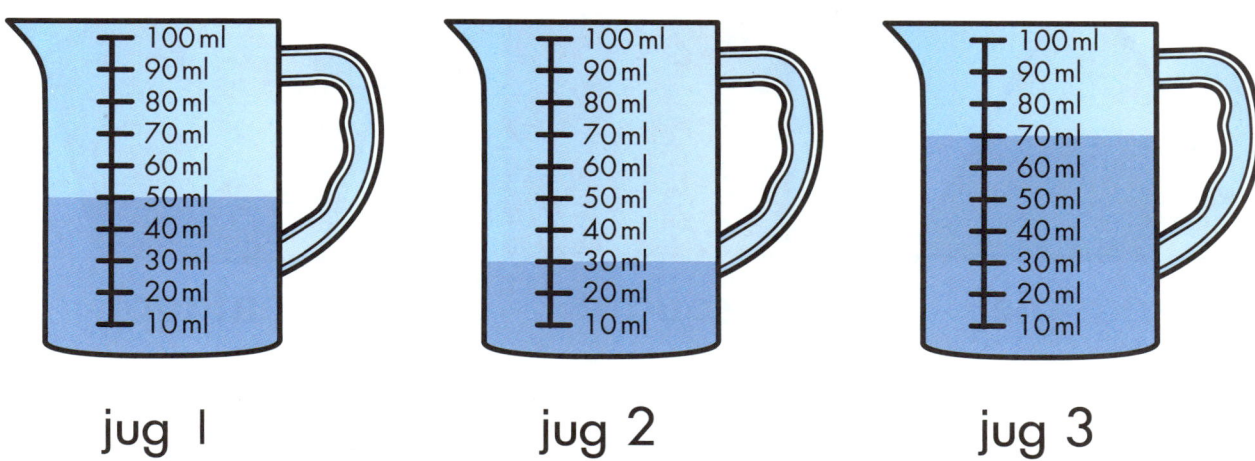

jug 1   jug 2   jug 3

Which jug has the most? ....

Which jug has the least? ....

Which jug is half full? ....

How much water would you need to add to make each jug full?

jug 1 = [ ] ml   jug 2 = [ ] ml   jug 3 = [ ] ml

2D Shapes

Count the sides and angles (corners) on each shape below, then complete the table.

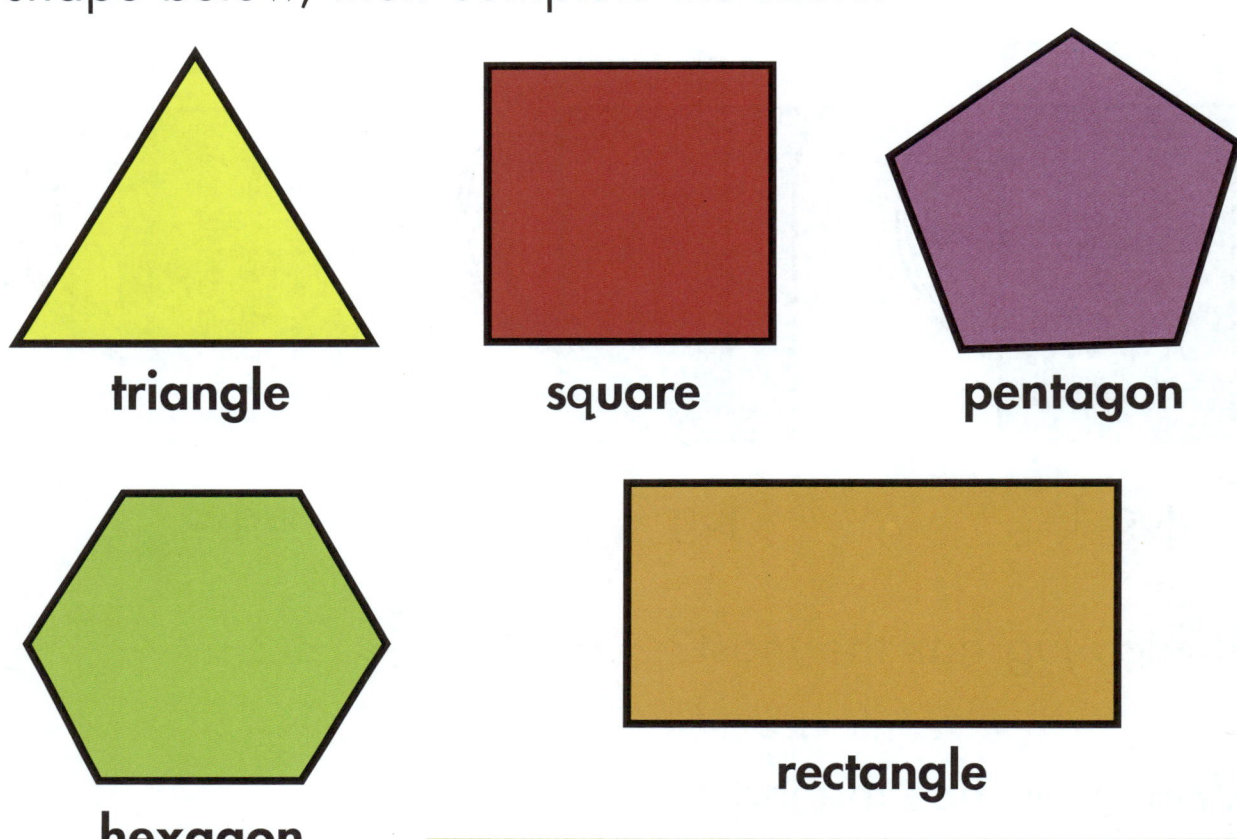

shape	sides	angles
triangle	3	3
square		
pentagon		
hexagon		
rectangle		

Sorting Shapes

Count how many sides each shape has. Put a cross through the odd one out in each group.

Counting Shapes

Count the number of times each shape appears in the picture.

shape	how many?
square	5
rectangle	
circle	
pentagon	
hexagon	
triangle	

Draw your own shape picture.

Count the number of times each shape appears in your shape picture. Color the picture.

shape	how many?
square	
rectangle	
circle	
pentagon	
hexagon	
triangle	

3D Shapes

2D shapes are flat and 3D shapes have dimension. Circle the 2D shapes. Underline the 3D shapes.

Note for parent: Encourage your child to find 3D shapes all around them.

109

Directions

These are directions:

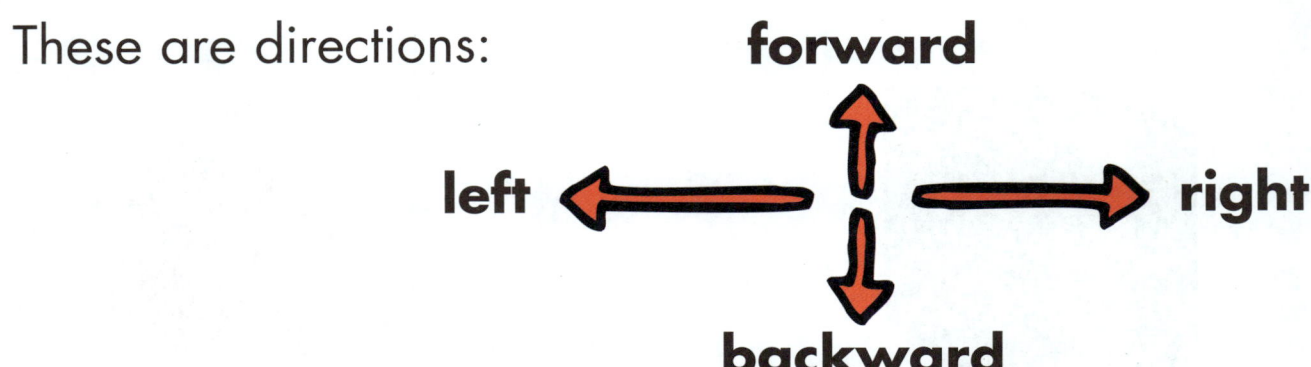

Look at the grid opposite. Follow the directions.

Start in the **Start** square.
Move backward 3 spaces. Move right 2 spaces.
Move backward 2 spaces. Move right 1 space.

Where are you? ....

From where you stopped, move left 2 spaces.
Move forward 3 spaces. Move right 2 spaces.
Move forward 1 space.

Where are you now? ....

Starting from where you stopped, move left 2 spaces.
Move forward 1 space. Move right 3 spaces.
Move backward 2 spaces.

Where are you now? ....

From the square you are in, move backward 3 spaces. Move left 4 spaces. Move forward 2 spaces. Move right 1 space.

Where are you now? ………animal doctor………

Telling the Time

Write the missing hours on this clock face, then write the times shown on the clocks below. When the big hand is pointing straight up it is something o'clock.

☐ o'clock   ☐ o'clock

Note for parent: This activity helps your child to recognize simple times.

When the big hand points straight down it is something thirty. What times do these clocks show?

....

....

....

Temperature

°F = degrees Fahrenheit

Write the reading for each of these thermometers in the box.

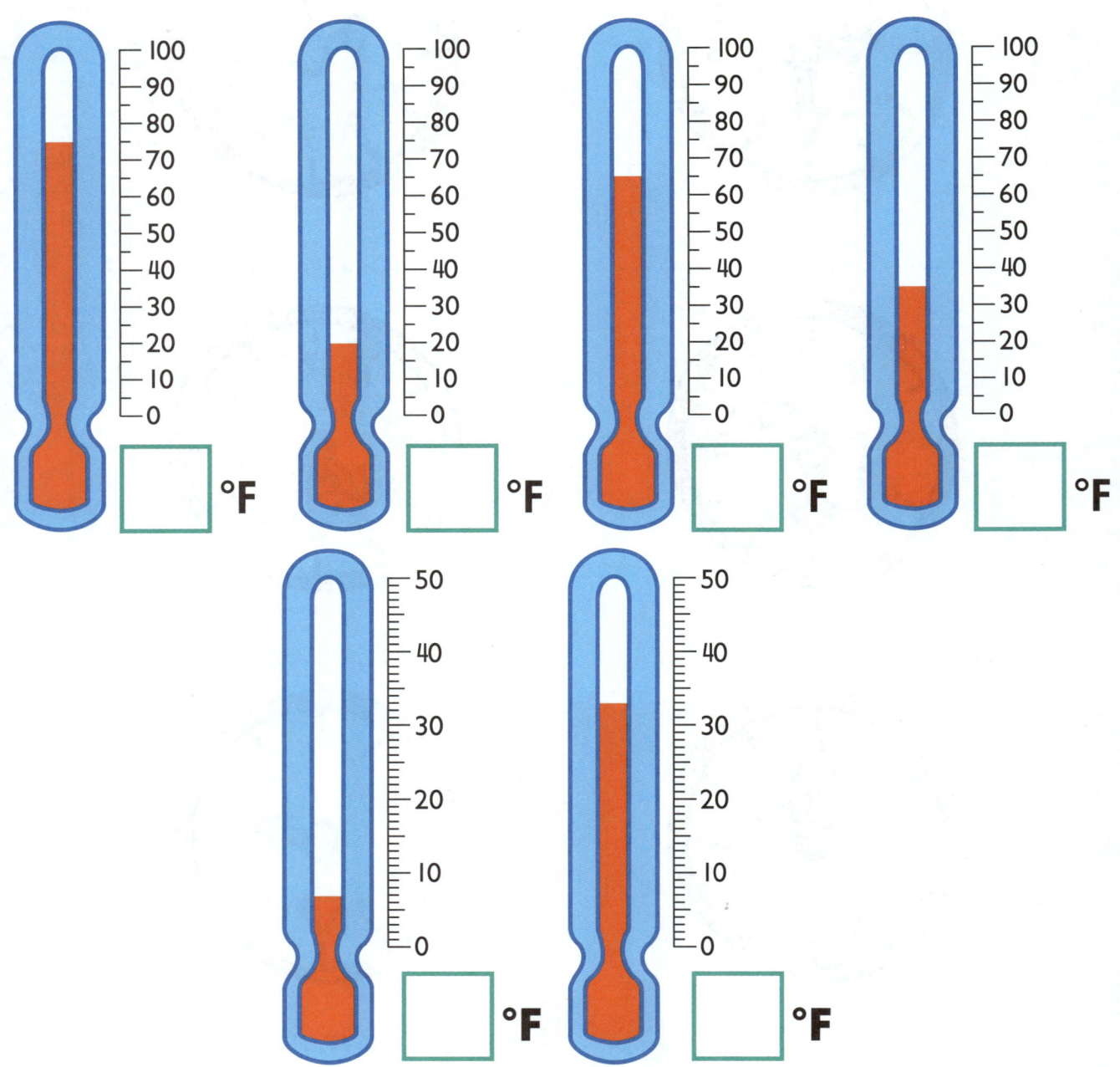

Color the thermometers to show the correct temperature.

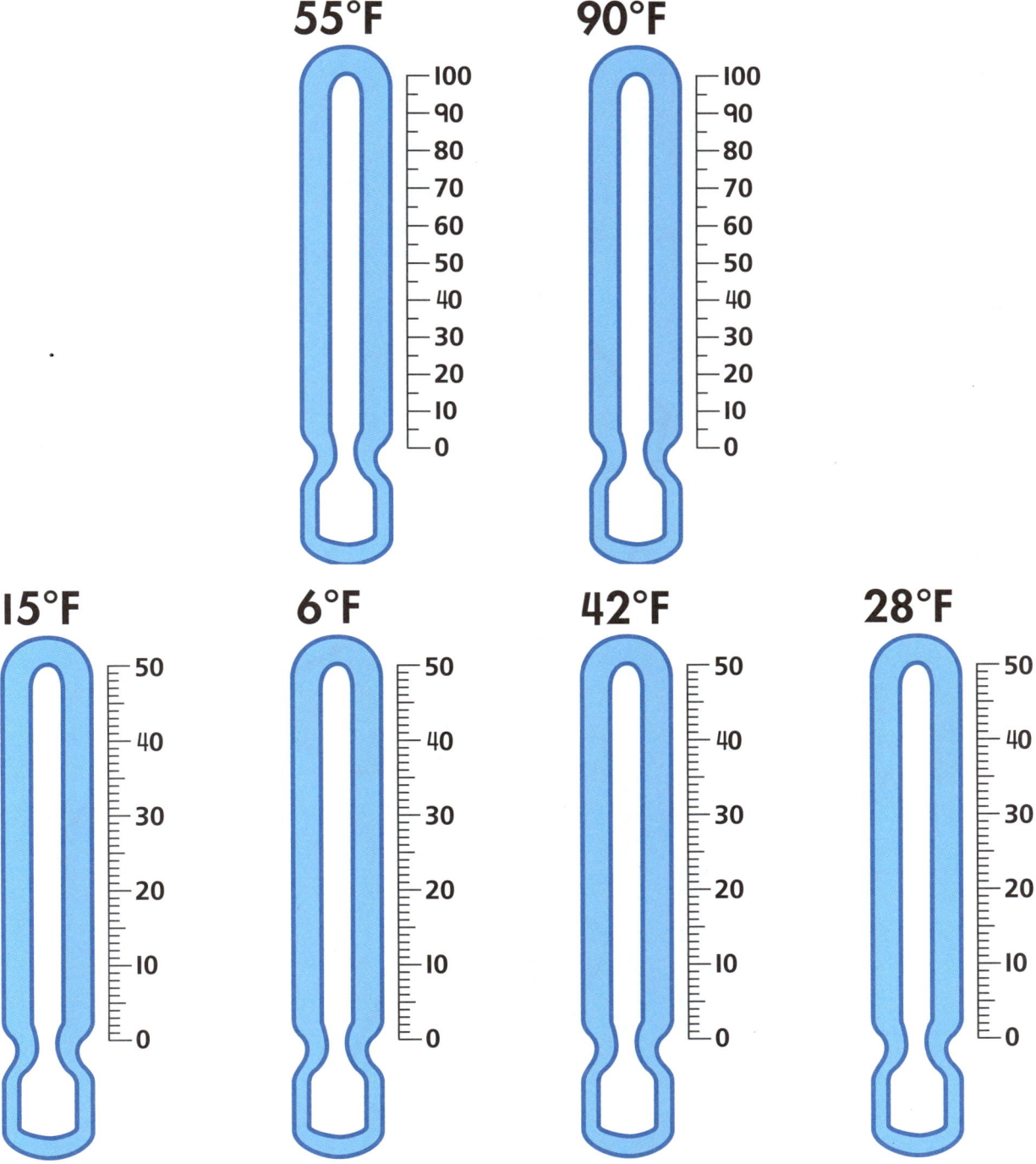

Match the Shape

Draw lines to connect the shapes that have the same number of sides.

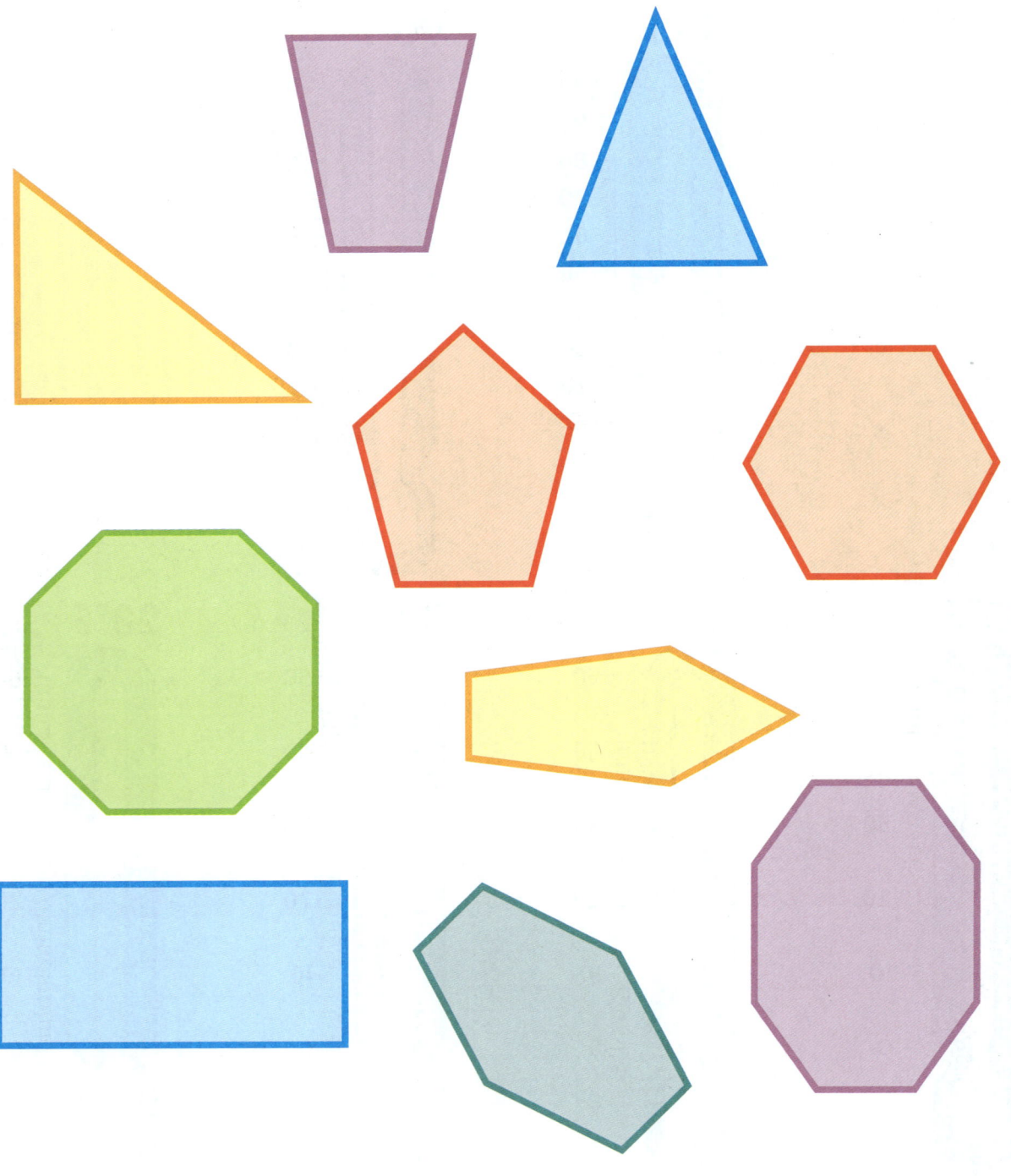

Draw Shapes

Draw a shape in each space.

triangle (3 sides)	hexagon (6 sides)
pentagon (5 sides)	quadrilateral (4 sides)

Note for parent: Explain to your child that a quadrilateral is any shape with four sides.

Properties of 2D Shapes

Write the name of each of these 2D shapes to finish the sentences.

| triangle   square   circle   rectangle |

4 straight sides of equal length
4 corners

This 2D shape is a ....

4 straight sides but not all are equal
4 corners

This 2D shape is a ....

3 straight sides
3 corners

This 2D shape is a ....

0 straight sides
0 corners

This 2D shape is a ....

Note for parent: Discuss the difference between a square and a rectangle.

Complete the table to show the properties of these 2D shapes. Use the shapes below to help you.

2D shape name	total number of sides	number of straight sides	number of curved sides	number of corners
circle				
triangle				
square				
rectangle				
pentagon				

Note for parent: This activity reinforces the properties of 2D shapes.

Properties of 3D Shapes

Look at the labeled parts of this 3D shape.

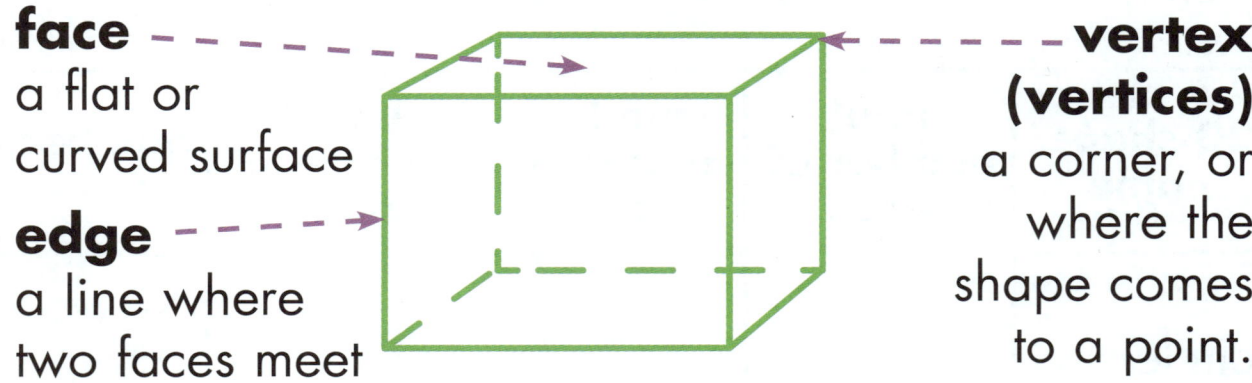

face a flat or curved surface

edge a line where two faces meet

vertex (vertices) a corner, or where the shape comes to a point.

Look at each shape below and count the number of faces, edges, and vertices. Complete the table.

shape	faces	edges	vertices
cuboid		12	8
pyramid	5		
cone			1

Draw a line to match the 3D shape to the correct properties.

8 edges
5 faces
5 vertices

0 edges
1 face
0 vertices

12 edges
6 faces
8 vertices

2 edges
3 faces
0 vertices

12 edges
6 faces
8 vertices

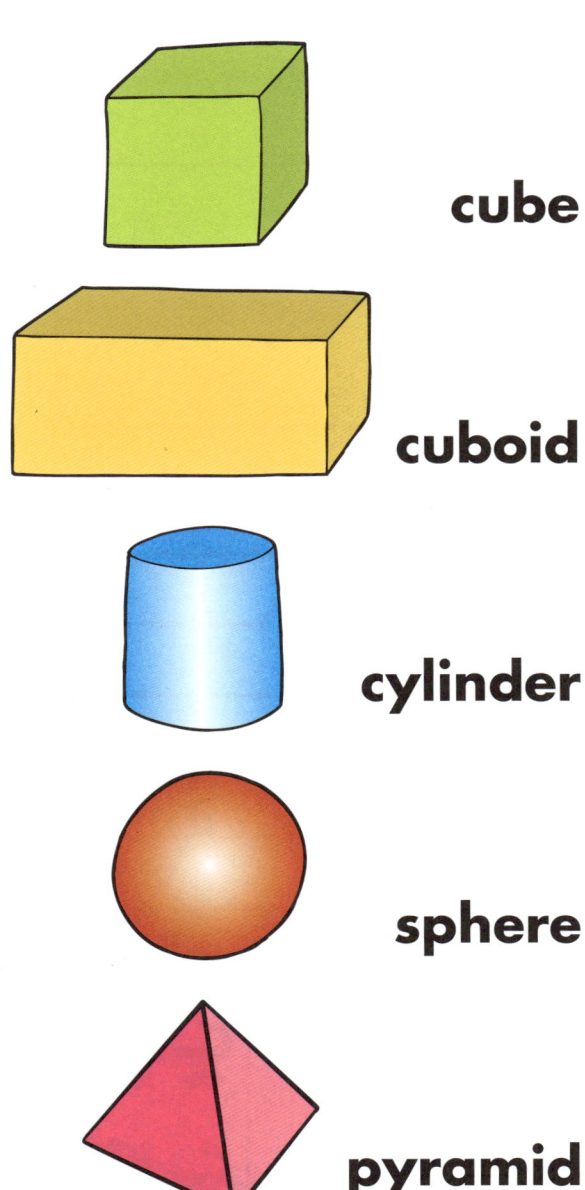

cube

cuboid

cylinder

sphere

pyramid

Note for parent: Point out that the cube and cuboid have the same number of edges, faces, and vertices, but a cube's faces are all square whereas a cuboid has some rectangular faces.

Tally Charts

Count the animals in each group and complete the tally chart. Draw a line for each animal you count. When you get to the fifth line, draw a line through the first four lines.

animal	tally	total
crocodiles	𝍲 I	6
elephants		
lions		
zebras		
monkeys		

Note for parent: Explain that in a tally chart marks are used to represent numbers. This is quicker than writing in words.

Complete the tally chart to show how many different types of vehicles you can see.

vehicle	tally	total
airplane	𝍅 𝍢	7
bicycle		
bus		
car		
helicopter		
train		

Which type of vehicle appears the most?

....

Which type of vehicle appears the least?

....

How many bicycles are there?

Answers

page 6
ball/wall, balloon/moon, bee/tree, nail/snail, carrot/parrot.

page 7
a (hat), u (sun), o (mop), e (net), i (pig), u (mug), a (van), o (fox), i (six).

page 8
m<u>a</u>n, r<u>e</u>d, p<u>i</u>g, s<u>o</u>ck, j<u>e</u>t, d<u>u</u>ck, b<u>u</u>s, b<u>e</u>d, l<u>o</u>g, fish, cr<u>a</u>b, m<u>e</u>n.

page 9
d<u>o</u>g, f<u>o</u>x, l<u>o</u>g; h<u>a</u>t, b<u>a</u>t, f<u>a</u>n; b<u>e</u>ll, w<u>e</u>b, p<u>e</u>n; j<u>u</u>g, b<u>u</u>s; s<u>i</u>x, p<u>i</u>g, l<u>i</u>ps.

page 10
bat – cat, fox – box, jar – car, dog – log.

page 11
1. ship, 2. sheep, 3. shoes, 4. shark, 5. shell, 6. shorts.

page 12
b<u>u</u>s, d<u>o</u>g, b<u>a</u>t, dr<u>u</u>m, cr<u>a</u>b, for<u>k</u>, c<u>u</u>p, te<u>n</u>.

page 13
sock/duck, brush/fish, car/star, switch/witch.

page 14
cub/cube, pip/pipe, fir/fire, cap/cape.

page 15
transportation: car/bus/train; food: banana/bread/apple; animals: tiger/giraffe/lion.

page 16
chicken   ship
throne   shell
cheese   thumb

page 17

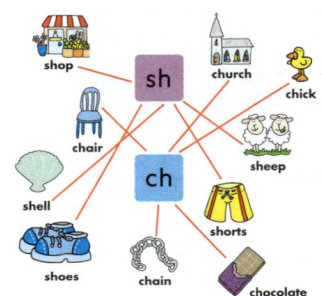

page 18
<u>sh</u>ell, <u>ch</u>in, fi<u>sh</u>, <u>ch</u>imp, tee<u>th</u>, <u>ch</u>ur<u>ch</u>.

page 20
Examples of rhyming words: dug, hug, jug, lug, pug, rug, tug, plug; bar, far, tar, scar; cat, fat, mat, pat, rat, sat, flat; den, men, pen, when.

page 21
clock – lock; chick – stick; bone – phone; night – light.

page 26

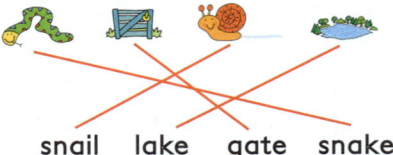

page 27
pain and pane, main and mane

page 28
head, bread, feather, thread, weather, meadow

page 29
strike, rice, slice, mike, ice, bike, like, hike, nice, trike

page 31
plume, spine, tone, robe, cane, cape, cute, huge, plane, tape, cube, tube

page 35
crew – stew – new – few, blue – glue, boot – root, noon – soon – tune – dune, tube – cube

page 39
The teacher is under the table – no;
The girl is reading a book – yes;
The boy is painting the door – no;
The teacher is looking at the girl – yes;
The cat is reading a book – no;
The boy has got a brush – yes;
The hamster is on its cage – no.

page 40
Everyone fell over and the turnip came out. d; The farmer saw an enormous turnip. a; Everyone tried to pull up the turnip. c; The farmer tried to pull up the turnip. b

page 43
What time is it?
I like to eat fruit.
When do I go to school?
The car was going fast.
Who went up the hill with Jill?
The cat likes to sit on my lap.
There are 8 capital letters.

Answers

page 44
elephant: A large animal with a long trunk and ivory tusks. It lives in Africa and Asia; kangaroo: A large animal that can jump very well. It carries its young in a pouch. It comes from Australia; monkey: A small animal with long arms and feet that it uses like hands. It lives in jungles; panda: A black and white animal like a bear. It lives in China; zebra: An animal like a horse with black and white stripes. It lives in Africa.

page 45
Page 18 is about giraffes.
Page 28 is about penguins.
Page 16 is about whales.
Page 8 is about bears.
Page 12 is about turtles.
Apes are on page 10.
Sharks are on page 4.
Kangaroos are on page 20.
Giraffes are on page 18.
Chimpanzees are on page 14.

page 46
Clare goes trampolining on Wednesday; Clare watches TV on Saturday; Jack goes to the library on Thursday; Clare goes grocery shopping on Friday; Jack washes the car on Sunday; Clare takes the dog out on Tuesday; Jack plays soccer on Monday.

page 47
Once upon a **time** there lived a king.
He **was** very sad.
He had lost **his** crown.
The queen **was** kind.
She said: "**You are** OK.
Come on – let's look for it."
They found it in **the** garden.

page 48
um/brell/a, snow/man, spi/der, mug, jell/y/fish, ward/robe, hol/i/day, oct/o/pus

page 49
A/li, Mo/hamm/ad, Ell/a, Na/zeem, Is/a/bell/a, Ol/i/ver, Jim, Popp/y, Kat/ya, Ha/rry

page 50
The book was about a dinosaur.
The robot was big and blue.
The rabbit ate a carrot.

page 51
Jan-u-a-ry – 4,
Feb-ru-a-ry – 4,
March – 1,
A-pril – 2,
May – 1,
June – 1,
Ju-ly – 2,
Au-gust – 2,
Sep-tem-ber – 3,
Oc-to-ber – 3,
No-vem-ber – 3,
De-cem-ber – 3.

page 52
duck<u>s</u>, pig<u>s</u>, cow<u>s</u>, farmer<u>s</u>, cat<u>s</u>.

page 53
1. ship, 2. sheep, 3. shell.
cow<u>s</u>, farmer<u>s</u>, cat<u>s</u>.

page 54
chairs, lamps, pencils, socks.

page 55
bigger, biggest.
taller, tall.

page 57
At the beginning of the story, Bella couldn't find …
Bertie Bear.
Bella looked for Bertie Bear in the … **bedroom**.
Mom said that they would … **find him tomorrow**.

page 59
said, so, some, come, have, like, little, there.

page 61
Who likes tennis? Zac
Who likes math? Zoe
Who likes science? Zac
Who likes soccer? Zoe
They would both like a book.

page 63
The porridge in the **medium** bowl was too sweet.
The porridge in the **big** bowl was too salty.
The porridge in the **small** bowl was just right.

page 68
10 apples

page 69
15 balls

Page 70
1 one   2 two
3 three   4 four
5 five   6 six
7 seven   8 eight
9 nine   10 ten

Page 71
11 eleven   12 twelve
13 thirteen 14 fourteen
15 fifteen   16 sixteen
17 seventeen 18 eighteen
19 nineteen 20 twenty

page 72
3 4 5 6 **7 8 9** 10
1 2 3 4 5 6 **7** 8 9
10 9 **8 7** 6
5 4 **3 2** 1 **0**

Answers

page 73
10 **11** 12 **13**
16 **17 18** 19 **20**
15 14 **13 12 11** 10 **9** 8 **7** 6
20 19 **18 17** 16 **15 14** 13

page 74
7, 11, 16, 14, 19, 13

page 75
7, 11, 10, 6, 8, 16

page 76
1 2 **3** 4 5 **6**
7 **8 9** 10 **11** 12
13 14 **15 16** 17 **18**
19 **20** 21 22 23 **24**
25 26 **27** 28 **29** 30

page 77
Both boxes contain 50 blocks.

page 78

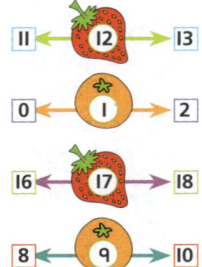

page 79

page 80
10 **20** 30 **40**
70 **80 90 100**
40 50 **60 70**

page 81
100 **90** 80 **70**
40 **30 20** 10
70 **60 50 40**

page 82
5, 5, 5, 5

page 83

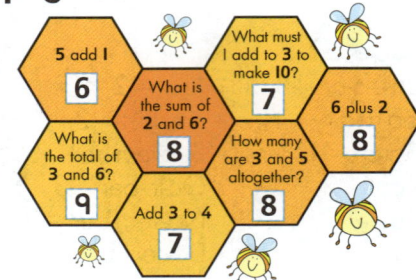

page 84
2, 3, 1, 4, 5

page 85
2, 5, 4, 8, 1, 6, 2, 10

page 86
10 beads, 6 beads, 4 beads, 11 beads

page 87
16 + 4 = 20, 9 + 11 = 20,
13 + 7 = 20, 15 + 5 = 20,
18 + 2 = 20

page 88
0 + **10** = 10   10 + **0** = 10
1 + 9 = **10**   9 + 1 + 10
2 + 8 = 10   8 + 2 = 10
3 + **7** = 10   7 + 3 = **10**
4 + 6 = **10**   6 + **4** = 10
5 + 5 = 10   5 + **5** = 10

page 89
10 − 0 = **10**   10 − 10 = **0**
10 − 1 = 9   10 − **9** = 1
10 − **2** = 8   10 − 8 = **2**
10 − 3 = **7**   10 − **7** = 3
10 − 4 = **6**   10 − 6 = **4**
10 − **5** = 5   10 − 5 = **5**

page 90

1	2	3	4	5	6	7	8	9	10
11	12	13	14	15	16	17	18	19	20
21	22	23	24	25	26	27	28	29	30
31	32	33	34	35	36	37	38	39	40
41	42	43	44	45	46	47	48	49	50
51	52	53	54	55	56	57	58	59	60
61	62	63	64	65	66	67	68	69	70
71	72	73	74	75	76	77	78	79	80
81	82	83	84	85	86	87	88	89	90
91	92	93	94	95	96	97	98	99	100

page 91
10 20 30 40 50 60 70 80 90 100
100 90 80 70 60 50 40 30 20 10
11 21 31 41 51 61 71 81 91 101
93 83 73 63 53 43 33 23 13 3

page 92
orange: 1 ten, 9 ones, 19 total
blue: 1 ten, 5 ones, 15 total
green: 2 tens, 0 ones, 20 total

page 93
orange: 3 tens, 1 one, 31 total
green: 4 tens, 7 ones, 47 total

page 94

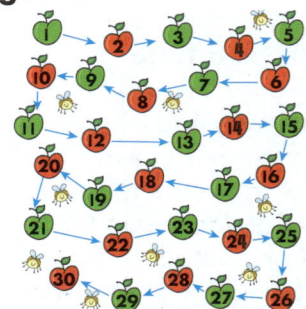

Answers

page 95
5, 10, 15, 20, 25, 30, 35, 40
40 bananas

page 98
caterpillar 6 cm, pencil 9 cm,
fish 5 cm, watch 7 cm,
true (the fish is shortest)
false (the pencil is longest)

page 99
key 2 in., toothbrush 4 in.,
fork 3 in.

page 100
elephant: heavy, feather: light,
balloon: light, truck: heavy
18 cherries

page 101
70 g, 90 g
The cherries are **lighter than** the grapes.
The banana is **heavier than** the cherries.
The grapes are **lighter than** the banana.

page 102
jug 1: $\frac{1}{2}$ liter
jug 2: 1 liter
jug 3: $\frac{1}{4}$ liter
jug 4: $\frac{3}{4}$ liter

page 103
jug 3, jug 2, jug 1
50 ml, 30 ml, 70 ml

page 104
square   4 sides, 4 angles
pentagon   5 sides, 5 angles
hexagon   6 sides, 6 angles
rectangle   4 sides, 4 angles

page 105

 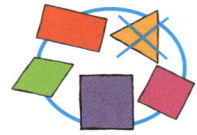

 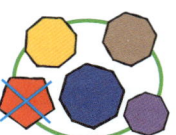

page 106

Shape	How many?
square	5
rectangle	9
circle	10
pentagon	1
hexagon	1
triangle	2

page 108–109

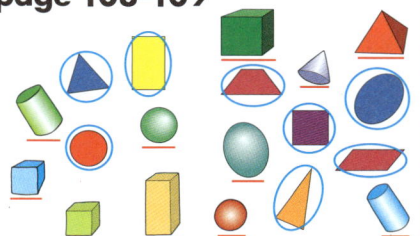

page 110–111
farm, bakery, zoo,
animal doctor.

page 112
1 o'clock, 7 o'clock

page 113
9:30, 10:00, 1:30,
7:30, 2:00, 2:30

page 114
75°F, 20°F, 65°F, 35°F,
7°F, 33°F

page 115

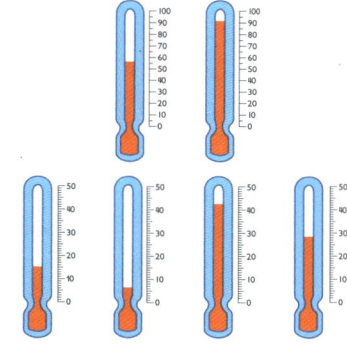

page 116

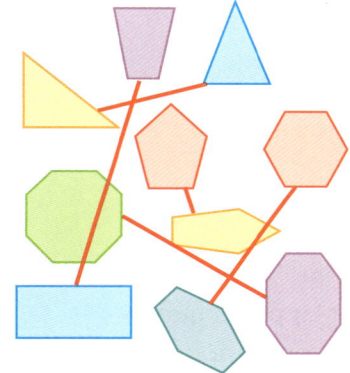

page 118
square, rectangle, triangle, circle.

page 119
circle: 1, 0, 1, 0
triangle: 3, 3, 0, 3
square: 4, 4, 0, 4
rectangle: 4, 4, 0, 4
pentagon: 5, 5, 0, 5

page 120

shape	faces	edges	vertices
cuboid	6	12	8
pyramid	5	8	5
cone	2	1	1

127

Answers

page 121

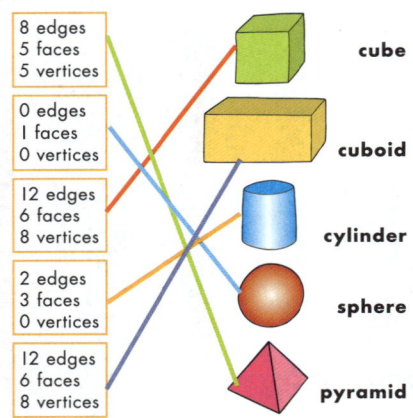

page 122
elephants 11, lions 15,
zebras 4, monkeys 9

page 123
bicycle: 5, bus: 6, car: 12,
helicopter: 4, train: 8.
The car appears most.
The helicopter appears least.
5 bicycles.